With Mouths Open Wide

NEW & SELECTED POEMS

With
Mouths
Open Wide

John Caddy

MILKWEED
EDITIONS

Published 2008 by Milkweed Editions
Printed in Canada
Cover design by Brad Norr
Cover art and interior design by RW Scholes
Author photo courtesy of *Saint Paul Pioneer Press*
The text of this book is set in Centaur Old Style
08 09 10 11 12   5 4 3 2 1
    First Edition

Special funding for this book was provided by Audra Keller.

Milkweed Editions, a nonprofit publisher, gratefully acknowledges sustaining support from Anonymous; Emilie and Henry Buchwald; the Bush Foundation; the Patrick and Aimee Butler Family Foundation; CarVal Investors; the Dougherty Family Foundation; the Ecolab Foundation; the General Mills Foundation; the Claire Giannini Fund; John and Joanne Gordon; William and Jeanne Grandy; the Jerome Foundation; Dorothy Kaplan Light and Ernest Light; Constance B. Kunin; Marshall BankFirst Corp.; Sanders and Tasha Marvin; the May Department Stores Company Foundation; the McKnight Foundation; a grant from the Minnesota State Arts Board, through an appropriation by the Minnesota State Legislature, a grant from the National Endowment for the Arts, and private funders; an award from the National Endowment for the Arts, which believes that a great nation deserves great art; the Navarre Corporation; Debbie Reynolds; the Starbucks Foundation; the St. Paul Travelers Foundation; Ellen and Sheldon Sturgis; the Target Foundation; the Gertrude Sexton Thompson Charitable Trust (George R. A. Johnson, Trustee); the James R. Thorpe Foundation; the Toro Foundation; Moira and John Turner; United Parcel Service; Joanne and Phil Von Blon; Kathleen and Bill Wanner; Serene and Christopher Warren; the W. M. Foundation; and the Xcel Energy Foundation.

Library of Congress Cataloging-in-Publication Data

Caddy, John.

        With mouths open wide : new and selected poems / John Caddy.—1st ed.
           p. cm.
      ISBN 978-1-57131-427-7 (pbk. : acid-free paper)
      I. Title
PS3553.A313W58 2008
811'.54—dc22   2007046471

    CIP

Printed on acid-free, recycled (100 percent postconsumer waste) paper

MINNESOTA
STATE ARTS BOARD

NATIONAL
ENDOWMENT
FOR THE ARTS
A great nation
deserves great art.

With Mouths Open Wide

With Mouths Open Wide

Eating the Sting (1986)

The Color of Mesabi Bones (1989)

Presences the Blood Learns Again (1997)

Morning Earth: Field Notes in Poetry (2003)
Morning Earth Online (New Work)

This Velvet in the Dark (New Work)

With Mouths Open Wide
(New Work)

I. Wave

With Mouths Open Wide in the Wave

Nighthawks swoop the lake with swallows and swifts,
all the fall migrants with mouths open wide.
In this dusk there is sky and lake, a black band of trees.
Sky and lake the same pewter, from the west a small chop
    of orange.
My eyes track one weave among hundreds, expect a rise
to the contrast of sky, again lose the bird in the trees.
All of us onshore are caught in this rhythm of
feeding nighthawks and swallows and swifts above water,
the easy swoop and drift and quickbeat and catch;
all the wide mouths take invisible flies,
and the rhythm of the whole is the ocean
at sunset, not the soundsurge of surf but
translucent, rising waves just before breaking,
when fishshapes and kelp fronds and cormorants
weave and flash in this same soundless
rhythm of nighthawks hunting a lake
two thousand miles away, both waters lit from the west.
There are moments when all that a backlit wave contains
can be seen, then chaos, collapse in confusion
until the next wave is made and crests, and the next.
There are moments when all the world's wave contains

can be seen, and the collapse is only the limit of eye.
But we know the world's wave continues its rhythms,
its nighthawks and fish-shapes hunt in their waves
and its leaves lift from earth in the curve of their season,
spring green from the bud, and dry for the fall
to lift in the curve of this wave we all roll in.
The birds now hunt now high as eye can see.

Catnip

Cougar locks her long eyes on mine, aware
she is only one leap from home.

I've carried the catnip harvest to Como Zoo,
a grocery sack for each big cat—my friend Bob
the keeper spreads the whole cut plants
to the Siberian tigers and African lions first,
leopards, cheetahs, then the New World cats,
the muscled jaguar of the Yucatan; our North American cougar.

The exotics revel in their tropic ways,
It is what I've hoped. I have given pleasure.
The tigers roll in it and bite and croon and drowse,
lions speed up to roar and cuff,
the leopards drape boneless on their tree,
and smile, extend their claws into the wood
over and deeper and over,
cheetahs increase their neurotic pace.
The jaguar decides he is made of jewels and convinces everyone.
The human smiles are catching and wide.

But the temperate cougar
nibbles some leaves, strokes her cheek in them,
sits neatly just behind the glass and
locks on my eyes, aware she is only

one long bound from home.
She knows where she lives.
She would not freeze next month;
our December is hers.
She can see white rabbits in snow,
and spot the grouse's breathing.

So we stare into each other a long time, a little stoned.
Things get so clear we both disappear.
There is a moment when the glass wavers,
her haunches tense—

Winter, Warm Blood

A greyblue blur so fast it stutters the eye
strikes a finch right off the thronged branch
and blurs a hundred feet
to an oak where it stops still as if

always still—but a wing sweeps and folds,
the goldfinch dangles from a clenched foot.
Flaps down to snow at the pond's edge
and tears, feathers toss.

I was going to say,
"A small hawk, sharp–shinned hawk,
adult: eye red, the fieldmark greyblue back."
Do that. Pull back.

The whole birch was goldfinches
waiting for sunflower seed.
Now it is white on white.
I could say,

" . . . the Autumn birch reborn with golden birds for leaves
is now but quiet winter bones on white . . . " Do that.
But the finch is yellowdrab and grey and elegy
is distance, not hunger. I can't pull back.

Could say, " . . . staring from a low
branch on a distant tree,
then hurling flat . . . "
I didn't see that.

Only the velocity of death.
I haven't breathed yet.
Was going to say, " . . . God."

Grouse Below the Sky, August

When they stretch up to pluck rose hips
and tender leaves, how tall and lean are
the fledglings foraging with mother.
In the open, one of the nine is always looking up.
They weave in and out of poplar and brush
and pine, on and off the trail's gravel.
The mother makes a soft continual cluck
low in her throat with her beak closed,
the chicks open their beaks to a high
piping that nearly can't be heard.
Above the mother's bright eye
the skin is a fine featherless pink.
The fledglings have grown all their cryptic plumage
except the fan, and all their legs feather
to the foot, the habit of the north.
At any alarm, the mother cluck darkens
and the young rush shadow, go still
and wait for her clear call.
As they work open patches, all look up
over and over, not a head cock—the whole
long neck curves to one side to look and look
well, as if aware a piece of sky could any moment
turn dark and fall in the shape of a hawk.

Manitou River: Cascades

The river oxbows lazy a half mile back, but a murmur swells.
The water at the brim slides black into chaos,
molten glass drops sleek as otter fur into white tumble,
stunning loud at first but a roar you soon enter.

Above, where water is flat, a few fish flies hover up, down,
flutter off, two waxwings sit an overhanging branch,
sunglow through their crests, a monarch flits the edges
among the fragment shadows of leaning birches, calm

until the cataract below hammers the ear, the whirl and surge
and leap into shapes sculpted from water ever replaced but
whose shapes remain through this season,
water sculpted by water-carved rock.

All down the cascades, rock-sprung roots
of small trees penetrate the basalt of the riverbed,
their slow patience returning the delicate leaf and flower
of mountain ash, birch catkin, cedar fan.

Below, a huge foam pillow rotates in eddies,
yellow-brown points on top like baked meringue.
In a stone pool on a rock between chutes,
air bubbles coat the rusty bottom algae.

All this water moving, always the spray, droplets
fling themselves over and over into morning sun.
The cascade's constant is power's crash,
the still pools worn in stone off to the sides a relief.

Water strider's boatfoot shadow
jerk-skates across the smooth bottom of one pool,
a mirror of six dimples from his small gravity.
He lives above this constant tension that never breaks.

Manitou River: Ruffled Grouse

He'd drum on the log,
strut slow to its end,
jump down and vanish in green,
run all the way through his hollow log, pop up
on the original end, and drum and strut
his way down the log again, feathers
large as the season,
and each time he closed this circle, he
untied a knot inside him
he had to untie.
The season feels familiar.
We trespassed on his drumming ground,
hiking through, and stopped
to soak in this music
of feather and wood,
this wonderful dance of male.
He saw us and exploded through trees, flew
right at our faces, tail fanned and
neck pouches swollen to purple, and
beat our heads with his wings until
he routed us, willing as we were to run
in our grinning delight, ears
slapped red and chest feathers floating
in our eyes, in this drum season
so lovely and knotted
and loud, and so familiar.

Manitou River: Forest Light

Light falls through cedars to
pool on the forest floor and lift
upward in shafts whose edges spark
as small papery butterflies cross
and vanish in shade.
Nothing glows like a fern caught by forest light
except rusty leaves, bluebeads, mountain maple
candles rising out of leafy spillways,
the intense red shoots of sarsaparilla,
dwarf cornel and starflower,
soft white dewberry blooms dusted with gold,
the epiphanic greens of mossed
stumps and stones and old root thrusts.
Only the weight of leaf shadow on all this green life
holds it from leaping up into this boreal light.

Fox and Hare

All fours, I scramble up
a granite ridge at the edge of sky,
shove through brambles,
scrape moss from its home stone.
At the top, I watch the red fox
lope toward me, tail proud, snowshoe hare
dangling, legs dragging, loose head
bleeding from the mouth.
Foam and blood at the fox's mouth
blend into his muzzle's russet.

Trotting sideways like a dog,
the fox sees me, stops at the edge, brush low.
Face to face a long moment.
He turns aside just enough to pass me,
trots on by. The hare's long feet
brush my jeans.
Fox grins. So do I.

Trickster at Play in Winter's Teeth

Raven tumbles from the sky, a black scrap
pretending the wingflailing fall,
and just above the pines catches
wind and throws her shout upon it,
the shout tumbles in its turn downwind
and lifts the fox tongue from its licking in the den.

Her shadow leaps across a muskeg opening.
One feather drops as she flies.
It falls lustrous, ambiguous, she reads her own sign:
a positive on negative white,
a taste of black feather for the mouth of wind.

High she hangs and plays through
white empty air, one bead eye
cast down at muskeg's vague hieroglyphs of winter,
reads the signs of wind working
on ragged black spruce and leatherleaf,
whatever sticks out of snow,
the filling tracks where paws and hooves
have pushed snow down, the long curve
of foxtrail along the bog's edge,
a sense of cold paws, ice building in hair,

a burst of static feathers where a grouse leapt up
too late, Raven reads the signs
and sculls through empty air.

Raven's shadow stretches across the white bog
from the tip of a windshredded tree.
A small steam curls from the nostrils
as she holds her beak high, chuckling.

Bullheads in LaSalle Creek, Passing Strange

Crosscurrent in the shallows, a mother bullhead
shepherds her school of fry. The story is already strange.
She is barbelled and black, only six inches long.
Her hundred jet fry wriggle in near unison, mother
at the center of a sphere, a black vibrant egg just
out of the egg which moves through water as a whole.

Shadows shift and dance on reed stems,
on caddis worms inching their stick homes along,
glance and are lost on old brown bottom leaves.
The grooves dug by clamfoot read like blurred runes
which currents elide just before meaning.
Swirls of silt surprise light on its way down,
make shafts of it, columns, as dust motes in window sun
make light more real and at the right age, sacramental.

Through these light shafts glides another globe of fry,
another centered mother. Here the story passes strange.
The two spheres meet and diffuse through
each other, interpenetrating like a living Escher.
As they slowly pass through, each sphere
keeps its compass, each infant its distance.
But the mothers break off, swim to touch barbels, exchange

what bullheads exchange, find their centers again.
The mirror passes through itself, current flows through all
and all keeps its form. Each wriggler in its world
tosses shadow to the sand, and the whole

casts ellipses on the sand and what we know,
but we do see this, and are joyed,
for what a wild order our eyes meet in this creek,
and what caring back-fence mothers,
as the shadows of the spheres mingle with those
of ripples cast on sand like old half-memories, dancing light
bounced to our human eyes which know little,
but open at any age, see so much, our eyes that do
remember light, and do enter when we see it, the dance.

Seven Ravens

Seven ravens play fly tonight,
five fledglings learn mom's tricks and dad's:
two weeks out of the nest they'll try anything.

We watch from above, on the crest of Wolf Ridge.
Small mists eddy in the breeze above the river—
it's twilight, disordered by the wild
array of raven voices,
praises and complaints,
love coos and laughter bubbling up
from the eternal fountain of *Yes! Out of the nest!*
Two ravens practice falling out of the sky as if dead,
wings aflail, and at the last instant,
miraculously come alive.
Wing tips cut needles off white pine.
All seven now hubbub through the sky, announcing
a death-defying performance:

One adult flies strong and swift downstream
twenty feet above the river,
another flies up and up two hundred feet,
turns and hurtles down, down, and just
as they must lethally collide, the river flier

flips on her back, wings beating, and grasps
the hurtler's extended talons and they fly
impossibly together a moment then release
and back into the sky. The juveniles are
raucous in their praise,
Well played! Well played!
While above, we yell ourselves amazed.

Grandma's Bats

Which is not a description of Grandma.
It was Grandma's cabin walls
that housed the bats, not her,
and she wasn't my grandma
and was long dead by this time, but
I lived then in the cabin known
in that place as Grandma's.

The first night I slept there
I woke sweating to a strange
chitter in the walls, a squeaking
and scraping of small claws,
and the next day figured out
I had bats right behind my head.
It maddened me the first weeks,
I raged, whined, asked around.
There was nothing to be done.

But in time, I'd sit out on the stoop
of a summer evening and watch night
gather over the lake, watch my bats,
the softness of flight more silent

than any feather but owl's,
the dart, the sudden shift for mosquitoes.
When full dark came, I'd turn to bed
and sit with my head against
the young ones squeaking in the walls.
How you guys doing?
In the morning I'd find myself talking to the folks—
Mornin'. How was the hunting?

Happy I'm Large This Night

Out watching stars bob in the night lake
from the granite outcrop above the dock,
we hear a rustling race through the dark
under balsams, something small
bounding about like a demented
squirrel, now here, now over there,
by the cabin, now right toward us,
some small life gone mad.
Night creatures are cautious, take care
not to be heard, find damp leaves to walk on.
I click the flashlight on to track this scurry
and the beam can't catch up to the race
until it stops on the toe of my shoe:
a weasel's long body stands
like a lean prairie dog and stares
up me as if measuring, drops
to fours and chases out of light, running
and rustling to see what scares up.
Eating surprised meat must be sweet.

Ruby Throat

Today the hummingbird displays
for the little female watching from low leaves.
Again and again he arcs a wide crescent
through air as if he were a pendulum bob
tethered by invisible silk.
As he zooms to each apex of this bow
he swaps up with down at full speed
and grooves air the opposite way.
Tomorrow they will both race through
garden sprinkler rain and its refracted bows.

Working the Fool

I believed the fledgling bird was ill—it trusted me, sure
in its ragged grace I would not injure it. At first I simply
noticed it, a plain bird—gray—and checked the yard for cats.
It sat among the leeks, on earth, huddled as if roosting,
    open-beaked.
Odd. I continued watering, spray wand high, soaking broccoli
    and beans
with a gardener's permitted rainbows.

Wilt and brutal heat all day—all sought shade except this bird.
It stood, poked about the lawn and in its center haunched,
feathers askew, eyes not swiveling for danger as they should.
I checked for cats, went about my watering while the bird
sat down on grass in sun and closed its eyes. It yawned
and hunched, and after straining open-mouthed, it shat.
I thought the bird was ill, but it half-hop fluttered off and
vanished in delphiniums. The dropping looked like any other.
I pulled some weeds, puttered and forgot, fingers working
on their own. Watering again,

I held the spray wand high above the herbs, caught my eyes
within these drops which rush to earth but shudder in the arch
that tangles light in time, like human life and loves—forgive me,
it was hot, I had no hat. The fledgling flutterhopped across
    the yard
to stand pink-mouthed in front of me, half-open-winged,
    and wait.

My forearm shifted the spray to this demanding child and
    soaked it down.
The bird just smiled, stood—no birdbath duck and fluff—
    open beak

lifted to the source of wet and cool. After a drenched eternity
the gray bird hopped outside the rainbow, shook itself, flew
    easily away.

Walking Sign

A late spring morning on a high trail
above Superior, soil a little muddy
and thronged with tracks
crisp in the sun's early relief
of hoof and toe, claw and tail,
clear as bells in the spirit
as mist burns off the marshes below:
splay-footed moose ambles along,
raccoon stops here
to check something out,
goes up on hind feet,
crow lands near this owl pellet,
hops to it, leaves it alone.
The leaf feet of
mouse dash through dark;
a whitetail buck
slow walks before sunrise.
The bold set paw of bear, clear
but yesterday, dry on the edges,
there his ant log, torn.
Many deer, more moose, still wet,

behind our bootprints
track us, dawdling. Then
delight: a huge deep
dinner-plate of moose hoof,
and in its center, a perfect, tiny
two-pronged print of whitetail fawn.

The Winnowing of Snipe

When I heard winnowing first,
I thought the owls had gone ethereal,
couldn't tell if this was voice or instrument
dopplering across the sky.

It's one of those lovely spring-male "look-at-me" things,
this winnowing of snipe:
to winnow grain is to toss it into wind
to separate the seed from chaff,
to separate worthy from unfit,
or "to blow on" as a breeze winnows grasslands.

Male snipe toss themselves into sky early on spring mornings,
or late in spring evenings, choosing dusk
to play with their wings on the wind,
to wheel broadly over a marsh where below
beautiful females wait and listen and decide.
The males beat wings fast and fast
and suddenly dive a long low dive while

stiffening the vanes of their wings
into Aeolian harps to make the enchantment
we call winnowing.
It enchants us and the large-eyed females down in the marsh.
Five or six males may compete at once,
to winnow the best from the rest,
or one alone may bless dawn with his feather harping.

Winnowing is almost a strumming, almost a song—
fuguing somewhere between woo and wow
across the changing sky.

When you hear it, it hums in you like the mystery
that hummed inside you as a kid—the marvel
of a sudden dip of cool air that washed you
when you walked down a warm evening road—
when somehow everything could happen
in the presence of summer and the absence of fear.

Flutter and Gape

All through the trees,
parents fly from their young,
who follow them like fate.
At the feeders, these fledglings crowd
the regulars like at a tavern
after the parade, all the anxious throats.

A juvenal rose-breast grosbeak
perches on the feeder's edge, sinks
his head outstretched and flutters wings,
begs all and any to come to him.
Grosbeaks refuse notice, done.
A daddy cardinal ignores him awhile,
raises his crest, hops over
and stuffs sunflower seeds
into the fledgling grosbeak's gape.

The Holy Indifference of Cormorants

July, near Viña del Mar, Chile

Looking north and south, the black line
dwindles into specks where
the coast fades into sea
and is lost in the limit of eye.
The line trembles, shifts in wind and caprice,
but replaces itself endlessly in single file
where I look west across an endless sea.
The line of cormorants flies close in
above the surf along this coast
of black rock stacks and chimneys.
Their wings beat quick sure scissors,
beaks point south, long necks stretch,
they pause for nothing, just fly.

When I come here early and sit on a rock
they are already flying as far as I can see.
When I unwrap my sandwich hours later
they still fly past the limit of eye.
The black birds make no sound that carries
over surf crashing on the rocks below me except
once when the line veers over me and wings whir.
As the sun drops into the Pacific, the line
—no longer single birds—continues,
same direction, same speed.

Awe can't last past these numbers.
They will continue flying in this line
all night or forever, and it has grown hard to care.

This line tires me; I have never felt so extraneous.
It is the birds' indifference. No hostility,
no affection, no notice. I am reduced
to the state the ancients entered when they resolved
nature into enemy—it wasn't beasts and bugs
and desert wilderness and seas which would not end
that tumbled the old ones into millennial war.
It is this holy indifference we will not accept.
But I stay and stare all day at infinite black birds
across the gulf we grew.

Sandhill Crane

for Hannah Hinchman

All the way north
her neck stretches to arrive,
and with each wing stroke her voice
haunts a chambered throat
with rolling horns we know

from when we were wild
and held to our mouths
the spiral horns of antelopes
and raised them toward
the flying cranes.

All the long way north,
the crane preens each night
with beakfuls of clay,
paints her feathers
so on her nest she will
be earth invisible.

II. Embers and Char

Embers and Char

Say you're in the woods and touch
char on a pine stump that burned
a century ago, rub its hard satin,
run a palm along hollow and edge.
Char is what lets the stump last.

Suppose the char remembers glowing,
as you recall embers, how they drowse
you to lost moments of lovers
hunkered to fires—tendon and gleam,
sheen of scar, a throat's apple,

the sweet belly crease.
Coals sing their heat, glow floats
scale to scale on changed wood,
shifts white, with a breath shifts red.
So we burn. Admit morning, the cold fire pit,

ash that forgets the shapes it lived.
There are still charred shoulders
and knobs, the bones remembering skin.
Char lets us last. Sure there's smoke and eye-sting.
Lift out of the wind. Bless the fire.

How the Tongue Learns Caution

Be a child again,
between the houses where lilac bushes bloom.

You have seen butterflies play flower here.

The small blue floret you
hold to lips with fingertip and thumb
accepts the probing of your tonguetip, then

. . . AAAAAH! Your body shakes, toes curl—
your little-kid cheeks pull tight.
So this is what coils the butterfly's tongue!

You probe for more.
It's done.

You become more direct, bite lilac
clusters off and chew them whole.

You have just grown up.

Your tongue only hints at before.

Yet the Sea Is Not Full

Last tide I picked it up by a wing and
spun and threw it as far out as I could.
Who knows why. Here it comes again.

The dead wings draggle up out of the wave crest
a hundred yards out, like a spent swimmer's
flopped arms that no longer know
if they pull down or reach for sky.
The sun burns into the Pacific, feathers
burn red on the angle of bone,
the wave crests again, the wings.

Yesterday I carried it by a foot
far up the cove, almost to the headland
before I threw it back.

At tide's peak the gull has worked its way to sand.
The head lolls in and nods out with each wave.
White head, yellow beak, eaten eyes.
Hello again. A creature of air nodding
pool to sand, ocean to earth. It has returned
to my fire five tides. We seem bound in a loop,
this dead gull who lost the air
and refuses the sea, this other who never had either.

The first day it was simply dead, and not my affair,
but it was my camp and I didn't want it here.
Now it's Huck's loaf of bread or something I can't cipher.

Out there in the rocks where this surf begins
kelp whips toss in the foam and
seals dive through the crest of a wave,
silhouettes in a green flash lit from behind.
The sun's gone oblate, burning to mate with the sea.
It's pretty out there. Here by my boots
it's a sloshing dead gull who won't go away.

What is it with all these returns? How long
can I refuse? Meaning is arbitrary, sure,
but the arbitrator has goose bumps.
What is more hapless than wet feathers?

Let Them Wake

In the center of an L. A. night
from the New Otani hotel,
I watch a man seven stories down
beat his head against
a metal streetlamp, beat
so hard it sways. Both hands
grip the post. Red smears where
his skull strikes a loud gong after gong.

Such music woke me.
He was mad.
I didn't go down.

But today all is mad. So
do this: wait for dark, find
near a block of cardboard night
a tall metal pole on a corner
in a pool of sodium light.
Make a music for today.

The grinning self-holy
hear no words. Let them
wake at night to our gongs.

Tossing Coins

The train full of Boy Scouts stops
but we can't get off.
A few people at the depot stare back
as we lean out of windows and gawk
through badges and neckerchiefs,
Minnesota boys seeing the world.
Here's a Chicana about our age
with her two little brothers,
a peasant blouse rides her shoulders.
One boy bravo
throws a coin toward her out the train window,
she bends to pick it up and we
discover her half-made breasts, their sweet points.
The train windows roar with approval,
a rain of coins sweeps out.
She bends again and again. Her brothers
run about to pick up coins
as boys from the train scream at them
in voices that break to stop
so they can get the look they bought.
Want and confusion.

Say I throw no coins that morning, say I have no change.
I stare like the rest, used to shame, willing
to accept it for her dark nipples.

Money and skin. And color of skin. She knows this tangle,
we know it now if not before. We do have change.
We have purchased so suddenly much. We are children staring
at ourselves shrinking rapidly away from childhood as
the Pueblo girl shrinks on the tracks as the train pulls away.
We are on our way to California,
    and the light across the desert is green.

Hold a Stone Axe

As I lift it my hand jerks
from the heat in this old edged stone—
as if the hands that worked it
just set it down here on river sands in sun,
the maker's sweat still
warm in the curves of this axe
which was ground into pure form
from jagged rock, shaped and rubbed
until granite was smooth as jade.

An odd comfort in this heat—not as when
a stranger rises from a chair and you
unknowing sit and feel that heat
against you—more like one you live with
has shared warmth with you.
It feels familiar, and plural
somehow, but this stone axe is
anything but new, the edge
nicked, worn by river and time
or use, or all of these.

Take its weight—we are together
in this—toss it in your palm,
close your hand on this clean

familiar shape that fish and bird evolved
to cut through water, cut through air—but
these curves cut through time
and flow through a darker fluid.
Touch in this stone the heat of all
these mammal veins, run a finger
where the arcs cross to form an edge—here

it would have entered bone, here
is blood of oldest testament, the urge
to shape an axe to split a skull—
and make this madness beautiful.
Such grace haunts our hands.

Nape Dance

Wife, through what stammers of time
have the small hairs on your neck
lifted to my tongue?
Through what slow evolutions and leaps
has your nape sought my mouth?

Mouth to neck we spiral down time
to when the pelt was loose—we are
so new when we're old—and taste
the nape's tang, dissolve the salt grit.
You are sinuous and furred,
your otter neck muscles up to my bite.

In the curve of time's tooth
our muzzles blur,
the bloodbeat of my tongue on
the pulse behind your ear.

Long before we walked the veldt
we lay secret in the small Jurassic darks
of cycads and ferns, and began love's dance up time
while the monsters roared above,
your neck fur always lifting to
my teeth and silent tongue.

So new when we're old, together we shake
so deep within time, outside it we dance.

Ceremony for Morning

It is the halflight pleasure
of my wakening hand
to find your skin,
to trace these curves
which bind your flesh within,
to remind your body
not of me, but of your self.
I touch your palms
and wake them into mine,
your fingertips then circling me
recapture me from night.

Gently we create
the other's morning skin,
and in this caressing
find our selves again.
Sketching with our hands
these separate boundaries
we bind each other close,
draw fingertip distinctions
until finally, all skin
is stroking and is stroked.

Tongue Duel

Before we are quite human, love, we are
children in a schoolyard winter day,
bright crackling under overshoes with
ankles cold as broken bells and chafed,
we are children in a tongue duel.

From the ritual of taunt we come
to dare, take angry places on our knees
in snow, afraid, and forcing blood into our tongues
we face each other's silence at the iron pipe,
frosting it with needles of our breath.

Stubborn, we extend our tongues to meet
cold iron, red tips shudder close to
catch the knife of cold and touch and
flick away snake-quick. A dare: we
thrust them out again, again until
we're stuck, tongues to freezing iron, afraid
to rip them off and more afraid to stay.

And afterward in bed, before we come to dare,
before we are quite human, love, our tongues are pale.

Sauna Women

You can tell when the sauna is hot enough:
when you throw a little löyly on the stones.
And the door puffs open just that much,
it's just right. If more, you know to duck.

Wet women in the sauna,
soap bubbles,
curious child eyes,
heavy old breasts,
perky young breasts gleam,
one pair milk full.

Wet women, skinnydipping down the hill,
careful naked feet soft from boots
always find roots,
but at the sand stride leglong into
the lake of night and deep enough,
squat—ah! the sizzle!
the laving, ceremonial plunging of hair,
squatting until goosebumps grow

and minnows nibble toes that dig into sand,
more ticklish at night,
spraddled in the cool black lake.

Stand, then careful up the hill to the sauna stove,
steady egg stones waiting on top.
"Löyly, löyly, just a little," and steam bursts from a dribble

from the dipper onto stones.

Dim, the small bulb mellows skin
as we plant butts on salted wood,
sweat lodge flesh, mother skin, grandmother sauna.
"I was born right on that bench where you sit." Jesus!

Shaping the Garden

Faded old women
in print housedresses
shape spring in the small backyards
of tired blue-collar neighborhoods
and dusty rural towns.

They bend from the waist
to networks of string.
With soft grunts they tie
white rags around stakes,
stooping to revived gardens:
"Grow here, shape green."

Look close. They stand and bend
atop a world's root,
a spiral winding down, on every flat
old women with bruised knees
engender gardens as
in Poland and Sweden, Eire,
Morocco, Nineveh and Ur.

When you step onto the spiral with them
and peer down the shadows
you see that far down the spirals
the housedress has become
hide with sinew stitched.

Barbershop Guys Relieved

Our hair drifts from us to the tiles
as the customers snigger and snort
and the barbers stop clipping when
the guy in the first chair
explodes the room with raunch.
Eyes at once furtive and bold.

Seventh-grade locker room, only
the guffaws are deeper.
That same desperation to be of the pack,
the same fear of being outside and set upon,
and we each truly in the barbershop
become one of the boys.

When a college girl walks by the windows
ten sad eyes follow her,
and the mouths, heartily carnal—
"God, I remember once . . . "
"Oh Jesus, look at those . . . "—
the lowered pitch you can almost smell.

A woman with a child opens the door,
and our savage, happy-together
tension pops like a sigh and drifts from us
like shorn hair and seventh grade.

Men and Swans

Men have no humor
for mirrors or
swans.

Men want women to be
swans,
and women are,
on water's effortless glide,
swans—that
bow of the neck, tilt
of head, the lovely
reflection's curve, but

Men are afraid of
swans
who step out
of the water, where they waddle
and squawk, crap
and squabble and

Enter water again to
glide the mirror,
big feet paddling madly to move,
swans—who
bow their heads shyly—the

Men on shore
unsmiled, calling
Stay on the water—

Who bow their heads shyly
and cherish the joke
beneath the grace
that makes grace true.

Balcony Girl

She was older, a dream fulfilled,
and supposed to be wild.
On our first date, one of us
took the other to the balcony.
I'm sure I thought I took her.
I'm sure she knew better.
The balcony of the State Theater
was where you didn't go
to watch the movie which
I don't remember at all.
I do recall terror and tingling skin.
She was supposed to have
a knife scar across her belly.
Story was, she got into it with
a carny girl one hot night in Gilbert.
But tonight I was the rube.
Her lashes were long.
After popcorn, she took my hand
and placed it on her breast.
I was captured in that
apple moment, afraid to move.
Something big was happening here.

2

Balcony Girl sauntered to the back of my father's lab
and stood hip-shot, me high on a ladder
painting the trim, her in a strapless, zip-front
summer top, the kind I never thought I'd see
outside a magazine, her breasts
trying to leap from their wired cage.
We took each other inside and teased a little,
pretended to bite, when my father
came in from the office in instant outrage.
I thought it was about propriety,
or work—I was getting paid.
She fled laughing; I was mortified.
In a while, when I snuck the door open,
he stood at the drawer where he filled
his pint, head thrown back, tossing a shot.
Now I know what she knew: he wanted her too.

3

Balcony Girl played country.
She'd tuck one full breast
into the curved hollow
in the Gibson's side,
bounce it once, look
up at me and smile,
grin at the crowd,
and when she'd hit a chord hard
the breast would thrum
gently there in its nest.
She'd do Kitty's *Puh-lease*
release me, let me go! and hit it
deep, a rich alto, the lovely
sweatered breast throbbing
like an imagined grouse
in my real hand, which curled
in the knowing that later,
later, I would hold this bird
and feel its heart pound,
a bird in the hand
to gentle and coax.

4

I was enthralled by her passion and flaunt
at first, until I knew her more.
She was tough, could laugh with
a toss of her hair and a hip sway
at the cuts of other girls' disdain.
I thought she was the essence of cool
uncaring, the most free creature I knew.
Like all boy loves this was about me
more than her; I knew her
no more than Hollywood.
One night after we sang western songs
with lyrics so corny we cracked up and rolled
on the rug, she grabbed my upper arms
and pulled me to a foot away,
put her eyes on mine and said
she was the loneliest girl in town, which
sounded, I said, like the song we just sang,
and she broke the skin on my cheek with a fist,
and wept and held on and held on.
She was tough. Her mother was invalid—
"bedridden" was the word, a heart flutter for years.
The house was the daughter's to run—
she got to take Mom's place for Dad, she said with a toss.
I couldn't contain then all that she said.
No heart flutters allowed.

Eating the Sting

(1986)

Winner of Milkweed Editions' Lakes & Prairies Award

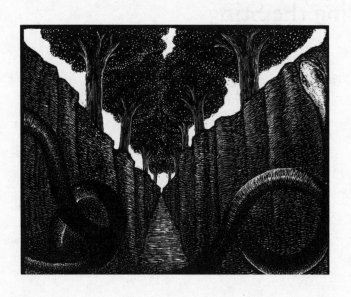

I. Eating the Sting

Eating the Sting

Caught in the snapped circle of light
on the cookshack oilcloth,
an upright deermouse holding yellow
in her fine fingers,
like an ear of black-striped corn,
a wasp I'd slapped dead earlier.

She stares, belly resonating, round above
a scatter of brittle wing, bits, a carapace—
she has already eaten the stinger—
stares at me, still,
something thrumming in her eyes

beyond herself, a mouse stung
onto an edge as far from cartoons
as the venom she's chewed into food.

She cocks a fawn ear now, trembling poisonchanger,
caught in the circle of light
I've thought myself in at times,

but never sure, I ask her softly how
she does it, if I can learn this turning
of sting into such food as startles in her eyes,
learn to suck pain into every sense
and come up spitting seeds, force poison
to a tear held fierce between my lips
and whirl it into tongue which sings, but

here I've come too loud: She drops the husk,
fusses whiskers with her paws, kicks
a scrap of wing aside, and whispers
thanks for the corn,

steps backward off the table
(and so potent she is with wasp)
flips a circle through light and
lands running on her leaf-toed feet.

Fisher Loon

The still glacial lake, our canoe
wake bowstrung through sunrise
mist burning off black rocks
thrust sudden out of white:

What is driftwood resolves into
a coarse circle of sticks and stems
under two large eggs speckled
brown on olive, around them slung

the long, smooth body of the loon,
flattened in the hollow of the nest
black and white, watching us
her wet eye——she snakes up,

drops off the rockshelf beating
lake into wingwater cast into sun,
stands on her tail,
opens her voice and casts for us,

sinks it back deep in our throats
(bright tears in laughter loon caught)
drags one wing half unfurled, tip
breaking the surface ripple, mother

cripple setting the hook, sculls back
to the canoe, opens her voice and
glories us away (and what can we do
but follow) until

far enough: the siren laughs, beats
her wings whole, shakes sleek
and quietly dives.

The Courtship of the Woodcock

Near dusk, the western sun outlining gravel ruts.
All afternoon he grubbed earthworms from the mud.

Later his wings will make song—no metaphor, real wind
through real feathers the colors of netted leaves,
astonishing warbles and whistles.

In the climax of his courtship, in twilight or the moon,
he will climb a helix written in the air for him, spiral
thirty feet straight up, wings trilling, circle
at the top and plummet openbeaked to ground,

a pattern welded to each coiled spring unwinding
in his genes, as this spring uncoils from winter
snow persistent under spruces, but now

near dusk on one of those back roads which lead us
to the wearing of a guise we take on unaware,

we meet him in the humming of the circle's finding,
not its piercing, where the river tongues the bank,
where the wave persuades the shore, as he walks
the ritual near puddles in the gravel road.

Somewhere close the female crouches, secret in weeds.
We are all most lovely not making love but just before.

The woodcock struts the road behind his downcurved beak,
the neckless featherbody ball perched on stilts,
pure seducer sparkling in his eye,

dropping one foot down from one long backhinged leg,
his body sinking on it to the ground and rising,
then the other stilt unfolds and drops and body follows it,

and up, the cadenced settling into ground and rising slow,
the rhythm of the wave upon the shore we catch in that suspended
moment when we in courtship first read in coupled eyes
that we will make love,

so the woodcock's urgent untimed ritual floats above gravel,
master, the held line of his body and long beak absolute.

When he stops our breaths go on with him, the whole
swelling landscape moves on with him: weeds, the puddled road,
the alders, spruce, the falling sun our bodies all
lifting and dropping while the woodcock holds the center,

the power, this pure possession of spring.

Bearwaking

I walk tangled in sun,
and the redwings dance willow buds
into gut-sung green.
Catkins drift into muskeg.

And swinging a stick
down an old logging trail,
round a hazelbrush turn
and there *Jesus a bear!* muzzle up
(slack-sided, fresh from the sleep)
eyes lock a long beat—he

wheels and claws flash white
from the shoulder roll gait
and I stand struck:

Drop my ear to the ground,
strain the pawbeats of that bulk
through the heart-hammered ear.

Roll over: a marsh hawk banks,
small birds skitter the brush again,
balm of gilead musk, a spider silk shines,
all the small graces tang.

I lie budded in roots.
There is pollen in my beard.
(His print begins to gleam with wet.)

Beyond Silence

Swinging open our arms,
beating them back
loud in the cold air
whitecapped and black, rolling
as our father evoked
flights of mallards
scudding like low clouds
over the blind.

Lake Winnibigoshish,
the slow browns of fall,
ducksback coat stiff on my shoulders
as I swung my arms.

Away from the shore, in dry ferns
I found on its back a whole
turtle shell and skeleton.
The legs were perfect, each
white bone intact and thinly held,
the links of the tail,
his skull, jaw slightly open,
neckbones curving back into the hollow shell.

I saw him green.

In the wind it was
so still. Saw
him green, tipped somehow

on his back,
waving his corded legs for days.
Mouth windsucking, neck
bow-arched against the ground,
always four legs straining
for purchase, the granite outcrop
beyond his reach but seen,
voiceless and waving.

When I touched him the legs and head
shivered and fell, the thin bones
mixing in lichens, leaving the unmoved shell.

Sharing the Cry

We cannot name this sound.   It locks the jaw.
It curls the tongue into the shapes
of sucking marrow from the bone.

From the pines a scream across the lake,
at first a woman's scream—but more, no hint of fear,
an endless wailing high and sliding down at last
to break on teeth and tongue, a celebration
of the lungs, a chilling song from somewhere
wet and warm, with overtones of spit and fur.

It shocks the muscles cramped,
leaves hands clamped tight around the paddle's shaft
and leaves the ear dazzled like the eye
by splintered waves reflecting light.

We cannot name this cry, but know
that this was animal, raw, entire,
and through the leaping drum of heart and ear,
the texture on our skins of standing fur,
we slowly realize that this was cougar's scream.

After, we hear no sound, make none.
Our faces pale, scanning shore, we watch
a heron lumber out of reeds, getting out of there.
We drift in the canoe and try to breathe.
We smile, and know one meaning of *alive.*

WITH MOUTHS OPEN WIDE

There are no cougars left up here, they say.
Does echo drain the marrow from the bone?
We know what's real: this cry
that strains our jaws to silence, and thrums
within our hollowing an old taut-sinewed fear
from the open throat of time. Without this cry
that curls the tongue into such shapes as these,
we are shrunken.   With it we are more.

Old Bachelor Offerings

He rises from the slough like history,
cattails sluicing from his shell.
The huge snapper rises breathing, bubbles on the nostrils,
gusty breaths blessing lungs
empty all the icelocked darkness,
since ice first sang thinly in November wind,
and thickened, and locked him in.
Sluggish he comes from the silence of waiting,
where the year slowly rotted
and sifted down to coat his shell,
where he lay dim for months like an ancient stone.

But this is waking: now
he pushes clumps of ice aside, black honeycombs
dissolving into sun and muskrats' paddling,
now he staggers through sedgemat and mud
dragging long algae streamers.
He is cloaked with leeches, festooned with black
twisting, recoiling from sudden brightness and heat.
He stops and gusts air, snorkel nose straining high.
In a straight line he flounders on, crushing cattails under him.

Weedslap: jerks his head in, stops. Rotates his eyes.
Old man gumming his jaws, he works his beak from side to side,
cautions his head out, and shoves his way up the gravel bank,
lifting his bulk step by step and sliding back, clawing up again
all pitted plates and scales the color of drying algae

beneath the frantic, tiring leeches. He breaks the crest
and gasping sprawls, clusters of snails huddled
in loose folds of skin
like an old bachelor lumberjack
in baggy longjohns winterstained
all the colors of a deeryard thaw,
who buttonless had sewn himself into them
last November, logged in them,
cooked in them, spilled on them,
slept the long incontinent darknesses in them
until they were both a season's record
and a second skin.

He sags at an oilclothed table next to a stove,
one bony hand resting in a net of sunlight,
chapped pores open to this heat.
His hand knows it is almost May
and time to shed the winter skin,
time to bare himself to sun
that winter burn from him.
The fingers curl and drum.

A flap of longjohns!
and he's leaping out the door
to purge himself in sunlight
on the matted grass,
He whirls barefoot among stumps
in the madness of Spring,

reeling at his chest
but he can't find the threads,
finds a rent and rips it wide,
shucks them to his ankles,
hopping in gaunt arabesques.
Like a boy he hurls up his arms,
stretching blue shadowed ribs,
and offers his paleness to the sun.
But his lungs cannot catch
this trembling air, he weaves
exhausted spirals toward a center
where he sinks

so the old bachelor drags himself,
abrading his sunken plastron with winter debris.
He knows this hurts, he knows this is laborious,
he knows his stomach is a shriveled kernel in his gut,
but he knows the sun is here and he has to get the damned
    things off.
He lumbers into light, crushing last year under him.

He scrapes and burns the winter from his shell and skin,
a trail of leeches, snails and algae threads dropping
as he ploughs another hundred yards.
On a mat of snow-flattened grass he stops to bask,

ragged legs outstretched, tendons in his neck
stretching the sun as it weaves from side to side.

With a hind foot he shoves himself in a slow revolution,
catching brilliance in the darkest pockets of his skin.

Enough. He takes his bearings
and lurches back along his path. Stops. Notices.
What are these black dying questions curled in wintered grass?
He noses one, snaps and gulps, and pushes off toward the slough.
He has made his offering.

Spring Swamp, Full Moon

In the night, in the ponds
I walk thigh wet,

A season's deaths layer the mud
pulling me in,

Frogs hang from moonlight
by their eyes,

shrilling of months stunned
alive, alone,

Cattails angle white in dark water,
flatworms on a dying blade—

Mouths, all the searching
soft mouths

pulling me in, a small and cold but
singing thing,

Bubbles of swamp gas laze to the moon
as I wobble and lurch,

From fall's brown scuttle,
tendrils of algae green.

Frogs are not mad.
The comfort in mud isn't cold.

Ritual for Hairwashing

The woman sits in her skin
on riverwet stone, leaned
back on a split slab of rock,
warming in the early light.
Her legs are spread to morning,
cut off at the calves in a boiling
mirror which breaks into foam
as it touches her skin, red
to the knees, everywhere else
loose with sun.

From wrists she thrusts forward,
flings over her face her long black hair,
and draws an arch with her spine
from river to stone.
Stares down at fragments of her face
dancing in the shadows of her hair.
Plunges her head into the cold
pressure of the mirror and lifts
gasping, she gathers and soaps her hair,
slips off the stone and flows
into the darkness under the mirror.

Leaps up from rinsing goosebumped and taut,
hands to hipbones, elbows akimbo,
and circling from the waist,
whirls that darkness in a gleaming hoop,

whirls it wet into comets and sparks,
voicing it now,
sound rises wordless
from her belly to her teeth,
and balanced on stones
she casts shouts in a ring to the sky
to fuse the river and sun.

Slows, breathing gusts.
Head bowed, her hair
sways across water.
She stands wholly defined
watching skeins of hair
drop light back into the mirror.
Shivers.   Bright neckbones
pluck the wet skin.

Ishmael in the White Again

As snow grains sift quietly from gray
overcast which sinks into the ghosts of spruce
across the white marsh,

As sap turns ice inside the birch and splits
the trunk and the muffled shot lifts nothing
from trees or drifts,

the only other sound the creak of boots on snow,
As nostrils slam white with cold each breath,
something above me answers it,

A great voice chuckles loud and twice,
a laugh dark as a dream's hot rag of night
answers all of it—there,

The raven, huddled guttural and huge
on the top bone of a tamarack, swings her beak
above a shaggy throat,

This black and stubborn heat inside the north
who knows tomorrow or tomorrow will bring tracks,
and flesh enough at the end of them,

Who croaks and chuckles and steams:
Rejoice! A furnace is the heart, and red!
Who gives a damn for white?

Taiga Snowshoeing

Still morning, spruce thick with new snow.
Breath is my only sound.
The first tracks I see are of voles,
delicate trails appearing
from tunnels under the snow, faint lines
of tails between bird prints,
brief journeys into night
which run five or six feet
and dive back into holes.
One visibly ends, a white thrash
within parentheses, the mark of the owl.
It is cold. The day is silent as feathers.

Suddenly between my snowshoes a partridge
explodes from deep snow,
loud drumming of wing,
powder thrown into sunlight—
I almost fall down, then she's gone,
crystals sifting over me.
A moment after, the only sign
a soft unshadowed hollow
where she sat out the storm,
and on each side,
the marks of her wingtips in snow.

Sky graying down.
Thirty below and hanging.
Two sounds: breath tinkling in ice dust,
and somewhere close
the raven scrapes her throat.

Bottomland

In a sullen backwater
of the bottomland,
black sawed-off pilings
curve out on the water in a long sweep
and abruptly stop.
Debris from the flood
clots the slow surface,
turning in yellow scum
broken by patches of oil.

I see a dead carp, its up eye
picked out, leaving only
the white socket.
The carp gently
lips the wet side of the near piling,
mouthing brown flood leavings, moss
and rotting wood.

A pair of rubber gloves
soaked black with oil
lies on the coarse top of the piling,
lined up as though wrists jutted from them,
both on their backs, with the fingers
full and curled as if filled with drowned flesh,
distended fingers and thumbs
gesturing, palms up.

Where I am standing the wind twitches me
the smell of the carp, of the yellow algae,
of the clots slowly turning.
The hairs rise on my arms.
I take part in these
dumb supplicating hands,
and below them,
the blind carp, mouthing.

That Humans Could Be Numb

At first through the startle I worried
that something wasn't right, that
needles through skin should hurt,
that something was wrong with my hands.

For days I displayed safety pins
dangling from my palms. I recall
a bunch of us in school, sitting at our desks
obsessed with this piercing, and at recess
scaring the little kids with our metal stigmata.

We were astonished that humans could be numb.
Witlings and naïve we were, equally amazed
at oleo and TNT, nylon, TV, titanium jets,
foilwrap, tunnels, rockets and bug bombs,

So we pinched up the green earthskin
from which we sprang, and stuck pins into it
over and over, goaded the planet
cleverly, idly as kids in school,
and didn't think it hurt,

As if in our making, some connection, some
essential nerve was never quite hooked up,
or fired so slowly that we
climbed decades between wounding and pain.
Something is wrong with our hands.

The Post-literate World

Just after the nocturnal exhibits
I come blinking and astonished upon "Tapir"
with an erection longer than his legs,
and hanging on the fence three punk leathergirls
in neon hair and safety pins, giggling
at his enormous member which doesn't drag
but points ahead at thirty degrees,
and as he paces forward the tip
furrows the hoof-battered soil of his enclosure,
but the tapir doesn't wince, just
paces forward looking sidelong at the girls.

I quickly move on, completing the circle of cages,
and find still hanging there a half hour later
the same punk girls, the same captive erection
scraping forward in an interweaving pattern
of circles made of shallow grooves,
under the girls' stare like some grotesque gigolo,
eye rolling in rut, parading stupidly erect
like an obsessive night fantasy.

The foreskin is reddened and must be sore,
yet he continues pacing forward, in his own
dull tapir way the quintessential New World male
who can only seed the furrow if it causes pain.
But these trapped punk girls, my dumb embarrassment,

all this is far beyond Tapir, who is simply
another caged, humiliated thing,
with nothing to spend his energies on,
the soil we live on too hard for furrowing,
too hard to expect much from our seed,
and all that is astonishing is that we continue
pacing forward, pretending the circles are not there.

Saltflowers

At first flowers, orange
tossing
over past the mint
and rhubarb gone to seedstalk,

the outhouse a tangle
of weathered boards
sinking, holes
porcupine chewed.

Orange wildflowers—strike
flowers—*butterflies,*
monarchs, so many
leafing up
as I bruise through the mint,

a weaving tapestry
clustered and fanning
in a wandering hole
so I hunker,

sweep a hand over, wings
fan my wrist, enough
lift and swirl that I see
they swarm a saltlick,
deep one,

deer-tongued from sandy loam,
a shape licked smooth
and undulant, muscled out
as whitewater carves creekstone.

The swirl settles,
orange on black,
spiral tongues uncoiling
into shadewet to dab
and dab for salt.

My tongue stabs the cheek
and wonders:

The craving.

Them too.

Healing the Voice

The forest of winter
night a gasp of white
stars reflecting sharp
snow and blue hands,
needles of black conifers.

welcome

the cold eye
opens in the yawn
which empties sound

can the sun be so small
can you so love the white

the glacial surge
of the blue wish inside,

the ending of sound
itself a voice,
here

be silent

2

winter forest light
bones rubbing bark,
rubbing snow,
drifting toward meaning

welcome

the snowwind fills all tracks, all
the vague hieroglyphs which
crook out of white
promises, the end of sound
a snow

healing the dimmed
edges of grousehole, wingtip,
of shadow chafed by milkweed,

the dragging pulse of cold,
the yawn

beneath the silence, the three
surrounds:

the cold pregnancy

the dream snowed in

the wish for white silence,
the return to the moon

3

the quiet of blue bone, the
closed mouth's
gravel:

tongue slowly bites
itself into
a white lace of roots

to filter the throat
and fondle
the half-swallowed stone

to keep the stone

to net the stone
in the cold slow chewing
of unspoken words

to keep the stone from rising

to erode it, roll the stone
in the lace, worry it
smooth

trees have time, glaciers

frost heave:
vomit the stone into light

red is the tongue
mouth open

4

the lolling tongue,
breath white, white wind, the
tracks filling behind

thin into a whine
on swept ice where the bubbles
caught in rising
wait

lick fast
the tongue will not stick

past the muskeg, leatherleaf,
past the deadfall gnarling,
the balsam gathers dark
under boughs, the root
curls into the den

lick
where the belly kisses knees

5

beneath the foot
trembling in its boot,
beneath snow, buried

deep before hoof,
hair, before
blood heat, below ice

the toad,
backed into dreams
of old thick silences

the closed eye knows
where is light

where is light
is there sound

squeezed into the skull
the eye will carry
the dream up,

hand will claw and foot
spade and shove
through frost,

the dream will thaw,
the forgotten voice will
pool and cry spring

fill the lung

6

hand loose,
the fingernail clicks off
a century of weathered
white pine stump

each cold time hard toothed,
each warmth eaten down
below the saw line

is there time

the hollow center
snow mounded

lichens sprinkle orange
rings, leap concentric winters,
nestle in the soft seasons

eat the springwood

under the snow mound,
dry needles, cones, chewed leaves,
old duff nursing moss and

seedling pine, small heaths
wintergreen

trust the center
suckle here

7

edges of spruce
split the moon's rising
and pull her onto boughs

her spending is white,
without wind,
swallowing darkness
in endless clumped flakes

without snow where is thaw

under all this white weight, all
the small crystal tunnels
collapse to april

melting, the wetsong, the entrance,
the beating shared,
the birthbite

again a pulse, still
the thud and surge of vowel
opens the dreaming of tongue

welcome
make noise

II. The Heronry

Albatrosses

The girl is alone this summer, more than usual. Dad is working out
of town a lot, and she thinks about him more when he is gone. She
remembers him once, when she was little but really she supposes not
so long ago, telling her about the albatrosses he saw on Midway when
he was stationed there, and how they could soar and soar on invisible
currents of air for days, maybe weeks, he wasn't sure, and never land.
And how the sailors called them gooney birds because they looked so
funny running across the beach trying to take off. He'd told her also
how the fliers thought that they were dangerous, the gooney birds,
how did he say it, "a menace to flight," and his voice had changed by
then, and it didn't make any sense at all to her that a bird who could
soar for days or maybe weeks could be called a menace to flying.

He'd said then that the sailors had to poison them, and when they
were breaking all the eggs they'd called the gooney birds dumb
because they didn't even build proper nests, and when she'd heard
that she'd run away with her hands over her ears hearing 'they had to
honey, men's lives were at stake,' and she had run and run to the field
and sat among the mullein stalks and all the sense she could make of
it with her face in her hands was an engraving in an old book of Joan
of Arc at the stake, the fire just starting, her white gown trying to
billow but bound around with cords.

Herondance

the girl discovers the great blue herons at their nests, and
discovers that to be simultaneously awkward and graceful is ok,
and may have something to do with beauty

standing on the ridge
before the heronry the girl
watches slow beating heron lines
carry her from distance to the nests

her arm drifts from her side

watches spraddle legged leaps
sway great platters of sticks

inside her boot a curling toe

watches lift and wingfall   furl
and open   tilt the windlash   furl

her muscles living shapes beneath the skin

sentinel   she slides an instep up a calf to knee
and throws the leg straight out

now stalks the ridge
strides arching up and toe point down

assuming beak she tilts and rolls her head   imagines
weight and fancies growing breasts and balancing

on stilts she cranes herself around

until her knees bend backward with the birds   finds
her balance for one step   and shouts her way to ground

tossing herons from the trees each open wing
a harp flung into sky and sounding in the girl

who rises from her clumsy nest
and scoops the sky up in her wings
to bank and wheel and counterturn—

but startled in her sudden grace   clacks her bill
and balances her flight with heron croaks

Between the Faces of the Light

closer to the nests this day,
the girl watches landings
high above her in the light,
and finds their shadows seek
her on the forest floor

great paper kites
collapse and collapse into boughs

each landing a falling
each falling a mad fluency

their shadows
careening through pines

fragment down branches
in tatters and flaps

come whole at the ground
then rush forward looming

and as she draws back
wink flat and cut through her unseen

Out of the Pale Egg Humming

under the nests for the first time
the girl finds the persistence of
death in the making of life, and
something of what each owes to each

she walks within feathers upright
in nettles like long winged
seeds twirled down from trees

is not aware she kicks apart a wing
of graywhite bones the shade of ragged asters
whose dark stems they fall across

she scans for nests and finds
sown high in spattered branches
light bundles of bone in wasted feather wrappings

a scaled foot a sternum   here a yellowed beak
obscure talisman nestled in the bones
like scarabs in the linen of the ibis

in the compass of her eye she spins
from death to hanging death so many discards   scrap

sees them all compressed   all
drifting like drowned sailors down from sky
to pendulum in shoals of green

shakes away this prettiness to search what's real
picks up a rib sinew curled around
holds a heartbeat for a moment
in her fingertips

and know for true the bough breaking nursery rhymes
with nettles singing in her eyes

Nest Tree in the Wheel of Light

in which the girl wakes in storm, fears for the
nestlings in the heronry, so seeks within the nest
tree a resolution of her fears, and finds in time not
exactly safety, but a longer view

lightning shot   upright in bed
goosebumps wind her toes into the rug
stands she now   gathering

the nests are in the storm

steeples fingers at her breast   lifts them high
wrists together   lets the hands
drop open   seedcase splitting from the seed

thunder narrows her

lets arms fall   stiffen
to the angle of the jackpine branch

window curtains whipping in her ears

she welcomes boughs   welcomes
bark glissading up her roots and limbs
carries needles to the edge of self and storm

calls up nest   weaves the old stick circle
knows its sag and bounce   to parents landing
taking flight   tenses muscles into nestlings' growth

a chill pebbles her with
thunderclap and rain   a glare   and she is

nest and tree and black in lightning's doubled night
of storm and bending   windcaught
a weight in her goes light   catches
on a branch below   a small flapping white

curtains in the black square of rain

watches time sprinkle bones from her
feels the moss she's tangled in reach up
to gather them   a greening of her roots
hears the jaws of small mothers gnawing calcium
to set their milks against the hunger in the den

heavy on her arms the great circle of the nest
heavy in her trunk new rings of growth

more lightly at her bud breast
the circle of the nipple and the mother's tooth
fish bone   to feathered bone   to furred

she sets the circles down and joins the bed

stillness   gathering

The People of Glass

Tell me a story now, like you said.

OK. You'll have to help me start, though, by pretending with me.

How?

Close your eyes. Get down on your hands and knees—yes, really. Make a snowbank in front of you, the tall one next to the driveway. Now make it early spring, one of those first sunny days when you wear your jacket open. Make the snowbank be melting.

Hey.

What?

My knees are getting wet.

Good! Now look where the sun hits the side of the snowbank, where it turns the snow into ice. See how it shines its way into the side of the snowbank a ways, so when you bend way down and look inside, it looks like a lace made of ice, all sparkling in the light? It's like crystal lattice, or like a net made of thin threads of glass. The creatures who live there call it the Worldcrystal, and it's filled with hundreds of rooms and galleries with shiny pillars everywhere.

The creatures who live inside call themselves the people of glass. Now the people of glass think they are very special, and in some ways they are right. The people of glass are hard and clear—they can see right through themselves, and they can see right through each other. Because they are so transparent, they think they do not hide anything from themselves, or from each other. But somewhere in their clarity they hide questions.

The people of glass know they are beautiful, and they do sparkle. Everything about them is bright and hard and clear. But the people of glass are cold, and this is a thing they can't explain to themselves.

There is a sadness in the lives of the people of glass, although no one speaks of it. They don't touch each other, or try not to. When they touch each other hard, they chip, so they are cautious. A bigger problem is that sometimes when they touch each other, even softly, they stick together, and can't get loose from each other, so they are afraid to touch for that reason too. And even the bright Worldcrystal they live in is dangerous, for if the glass people don't keep constantly moving, they find themselves stuck to the floor or walls, so they think the smart thing to do is to always keep moving and never stop. There are some stuck ones reaching out to touch them as they constantly walk and walk, who remind them to always keep moving.

Bend down again and look way inside—see the sparkling? That's them. They're moving so fast all you can see is the sparkle.

So the people of glass keep moving, and they think they know why. But the people of glass don't touch each other, and this too is a thing they can't explain to themselves. They are afraid to touch and afraid to stop moving, just plain scared, but they call it being sensible, common sense that any fool could understand.

One of the fools who couldn't quite understand was a girl named Winterrain. Unlike most of the glass people, she found herself pulled toward the Great Light at the front of the Worldcrystal. She liked very much to go there, even though when she did, and touched her face, it was wet, like she was weeping, and this confused her, because the people of glass were hard and did not know what weeping was.

But even so she found some great pleasure in the Light, some feeling that there was more to life than endlessly walking and walking to keep from getting stuck.

After Winterrain had gone to the strongest part of the Light many times, she saw that inside her clear body she had developed a network of fine cracks. This frightened her, but it somehow seemed natural to her. Most of the people of glass jeered when they saw her fine cracks, and made fun of her, because she wasn't quite clear anymore. But a few of them found her beautiful, because of the way light would reflect off the cracks and bounce around inside her body. It was like she carried some of the Great Light around inside her now.

To those who found her beautiful, Winterrain confided that she was learning to understand about the people of glass, and she did this quietly, because what she was learning was frightening. But she told those few the truth she was finding out by going to the Light: that they were not the people of glass at all—they were the people of ice. That they were hiding from themselves the fact that they could melt.

Now this was scary news. Can you imagine the sparkling and gleaming when they heard? Winterrain also told them that if they touched and joined together, they would live longer and last better in the Light, even though eventually they might still melt away. But by then her friends had become so scared by her words that they ran away, and by then, Winterrain was stuck. From then on, everyone who passed mocked her, poor cracked Winterrain, and called her soft, and other glass people insults—and it was true that she was no longer quite clear, and no longer very hard.

Then, quite suddenly, the Sun hung low on the horizon one day and reached far inside the Worldcrystal, and all the glass people melted in their tracks, even poor cracked Winterrain with light bouncing all around inside her, and as she melted, she understood her name.

What kind of story is that? Everyone dies and it doesn't mean anything!

Wait. I'm not done yet. You see, when the people of glass, who were really of ice, when they melted, they all turned into little puddles of water, and the puddles eventually became part of everything in the whole world. Some became part of the birds who came with spring and drank from them, and flew away without their thirst. And some became part of a small pond where the frogs came and sang strange songs all night. Many sank into the earth and found seeds to swell, and those became part of the grasses and wildflowers of the field, and watched the moonlit rabbits dance. And Winterrain, the special one, the one who found out the truth about herself? The puddle of her melting was lifted up into the sky by the Sun, the Great Light, and became part of the air, the air you are breathing as you listen to this tale. So now she is inside you, and touching you, and part of you—and if you are lucky, Winterrain will help you to see what you are.

Wild Canaries

Up to the high pasture this morning, in the August buzz of grasses
gone to seedheads hanging over sorrel reddening, only the tallest
toughest flowers open now, even the thousand thistles turned now
from cobalt to white, and she expects when she reaches the crest a sea
of thistle white sprinkled with tobacco stalks of dock and mullein
spears still blooming yellow at their tips. As she hikes uphill each
step creates a dusty surge of grasshoppers, green ones leaping, the grey
kind unfolding black and yellow wings, hard to see until, all clicking
as they move, and above them dragonflies with tails of red and powder
blue and green, and it is August, but it feels to her like beginnings.

At the crest where she thinks *Now white, a sea of white,* at the crest a
froth of gold, goldfinches every-which-angled on white thistles, and in
the sunlight like gauze is thistledown floating everywhere, and finches
ride the seedheads, singly dancing across the field like the small chop
and dither of water on top of the flock's deeply swelling wave which
advances on her as she stands amazed. First a white puffed thistlehead,
then a sudden bent and golden bloom which pulls each bit of fluff
from its seed and tosses what is left onto the breeze as children do
the milkweed pods, then off to light on another, all these goldfinches
dip and lift and fall, and as they rise each sings. All around her now
the flock, parting an arm's length on either side, and she thinks of
schooling minnows in the shallows parting for her ankles. The flock
moves slowly through her as a sun-chopped wave, slowly, one that's
come all distances and more and unready yet to break. *Oh, their slow
surrounding swell*—she names it *Thistle speed,* and *This day, this day,* she

says, *is gold,* and in the breeze the thistles rise and dip, and her knees dip and rise, and the finches lift and fall and lift, and as they rise they sing.

It feels to the girl like beginnings, or is it something endless, something of great circles and of waves, swelling gentle waves circling time for century after century but always new, renewed, and she is in it, of it, adrift on this golden day of finches and of thistledown, wondering still as her knees dip and rise how something endless can feel so like beginnings.

The White Dream

In her dream are two figures, a white eagle and a man. And herself, a girl hanging back or just a watching thought. They are in a boundless white space, all featureless and white, except for a green oak and the scarlet clothing of the man.

The white eagle is soaring and swooping incredibly, testing the limits of flight, now straining so high it is lost, now dropping, expanding with a rush of black talons. But the man is its master, he has trained it, and the white eagle flies on the tether of his eyes. The man watches the performance, commands rolls, circles left, circles right with theatrical gestures of the hand. The white eagle whirls and spins in the air like an ice skater. The girl's lips do not move but she hears her voice demand, *Why would an eagle do that for you?* The man glances at her, as if he had known she were watching, turns his eyes back to the spinning eagle and replies, *For promises.*

When the dream dissolves it sticks with her, uncomfortably. She does not know what it means. She finds herself replaying it.

On the Day of Wind

The sentinel herons ride thin treetops which pitch and roll ten feet from side to side, wings held crook'd and knees sharply backbent, long toes curled around pinebark like huge redwings clinging to fifty foot cattails. One rides a tree for a time, then uncurls his toes and without moving wings sails to a treetop twenty feet away, toe-hooking a branch—then again, again, island hopping.

Today nothing has its neck pulled in, today everyone flies without working: the windknocked raven banking from a kamikaze blackbird, the high fishstealing eagle, circling. Herons whip by like great tornloose sails, turn and hang still for improbable moments.

Gusts toss the heronry clatter in and out of the girl's ears. A fleet of tall cumulus sails in blue distance beyond the rafted nests tossing in the clear. Returning herons board the nests like pirates boarding galleons, gripping the gunwales and flapping, croaking while the passengers jabber back, swaying precariously as their swords dive deep into the confusion of yellow beaks.

Fifty feet below, tethered to the seafloor, the girl rides her tiptoes.

The Color of Mesabi Bones
(1989)

Winner of the Los Angeles Times Book Prize
&
Minnesota Book Award

A Lozenge

The child remains always
dangerous, alive but
blunted until a man's absent

tongue worries a key out
from some pocket
of memory and rolls it
over in the mouth, a lozenge of

whispers, of hair in firelight,
a mother's hand shifting
from cookstove to forehead, of
elephants straining to canvas,
locomotives' night steaming,

gypsy wagons, tricycle bells . . . rolls it
over until breath opens and eyes enlarge
and the child yawns,
waking—when the guilty start

stops it, the key
quickly swallowed, jaw
hardened, eyes again small, the man
resumed.

St. Austell, Cornwall

Great-grandfather Coad went into the mine
at six years of age. Stretching his thin legs to
reach iron rungs a full foot apart.
apprenticed to his dad, listening to the ore carts'
wheels rolling echoes up and down
the hollowed fossil sea.

For a thousand days just before dawn he turned
his pale eyes toward the sea, stepped onto the ladders
and lowered his body down the deep shaft.
The Cornish need sea, wet or turned rock,
mine drifts and beach dunes the saltsame smell.
Before that boy was done he'd carved holes
in the bones of three fossil oceans.

Orphaned at nine, he smuggled his minewhite
skin into the hold of a freighter America bound,
as his fathers dreamed of embarking
for the Summer Country or Avalon, dreaming
always West as they smuggled and mined.

He crept into the hold, trading dark for dark,
found a hollow in crates and listened to cargo
roll and thump in the waves of the living Atlantic,

Boyman, a miner, missing the pasties his mother
would tuck into his shirt,
fingering the threads where she patched it.

A miner born, or made by nine, stowaway.
What could his children expect?
What would they grow at the other end of this sea?

Mine Towns

Much abandoned now, forced out or grown over, gone,
thrown into memory's hole. You have to dig for it.
Water-filled pits, rusted washing plants and crushers.
Tracks and spurs that just stop. The white pine cut,
the iron dug out. Not even much red left. No dust
coating cars or ground into hands. But bones mix with ore
in these empty mines, and the bones are red.

Much has always died. Towns: old Mesaba, Adriatic, Elcor.
Old pavement weedsplit. Lost customs and recipes,
causes and countries. Words: *Poyka. Sisu.* Short old women
in black babushkas clumped in front of churches.
Sayings: *May the Devil carry you off in a sack!*
Whole languages: Serb, French, Italian, stubborn Finn,
merchants who could speak them.

Much has died. Some still nourishes. Strike dreams:
1907, the Wobblies in '16, the thirties, fifties—dreams
of a living wage, justice, victory. Lost homesteads and saunas,
Finnish dovetails still wedging the squared white pine.
Logging camps: a privy, a chimney half-standing.

Some refuses death: time-warp Friday nights
on Chestnut Street, bumper to cruising bumper, sidewalks
swirling, all the bars bright, everyone calling *Hey*
to everyone, the polka lilt to the voice and the eye.
Behind town, out in the woods in old jackpine slash,

WITH MOUTHS OPEN WIDE

polished cones grip their seeds like gray stones,
wait lifespans for the fire to bloom.

Much is buried for the digging. The Mill Forty:
tangled concrete roots of the world's largest sawmill.
Sprinkled through fields where the company
moved the houses off, open cellars choked with raspberries.
By the back steps, rhubarb still thrusts its spear,
comfrey sprawls, mints and lilies struggle with long grass.

Abandoned now, knocked down and forced out, thrown
into memory's hole, the shaft leading to the full heart
where it all and always is embraced and laugh-angry and alive.

Shaken Child

The doctor slides the X-rays from manila,
clips them to the fluorescent wall
and I am seized in giant's hands and shaken into
two—*Look*—*these concretions here, the black*
lumps—bone burned into acetate—
notice the arm bones—*would appear*
that damage early—the giant squeezes
hard fingers around our bones, the child
holds—as a whipped dog presents its
throat—quiet, holds still to invoke
the rule of submission, hoping
rather awkward to say the doctor
murmurs *damage to the cervical vertebrae* . . .
the giant with small eyes shakes the child's
head a popping doll's head on a spring,
Calcareous knots on the bones, yes
this black but really white of course, a
negative—this is what the bones and meat
have always known—*We can't be*
optimistic, the injuries are old—*with*
patience perhaps? the arms the neck—the
buried child opening—*An X-ray syndrome*
. . . shaken child . . . we can't be sure
of course . . . I am sure. Finally. Wait
for all to stop so we can
breathe, wait to master stillness no

expression, hoping while the child
swells into now and fugues the giant's
always first words, *Don't give me that*
look! his sudden lunge, the chase—shaken
man, shaken child who never knew
the rules, or when the game began, or
even the number of players,
and I sit unmoving on the doctor's chair.

The War Effort

After supper I'd use the can opener to cut the bottoms off the day's
tin cans, slip the two end circles inside the open cylinder, place them
on the linoleum, and—freedom of noisy freedoms!—stamp them
flat. What could he say? They were for the War Effort. We were all
Patriots. We had Drives: paper, scrap metal, old tires.

We carried dimes in our mittens to grade school to slowly buy Bonds.
The teachers sold us small red stamps with the Concord Minuteman
on them, and we'd lick them into books.
A full book meant—the teachers always said it in full—a United
States War Bond. We figured a jeep, maybe even a tank's worth.

We learned to talk in Capitals. We had Drives and Victory Gardens,
Blackouts and Spies. Victory Gardens, I knew, had to make a "V"
shape in the earth or they wouldn't help the war.

Spies were all around. The mines were Targets. Once we saw a spy in
a Piper Cub flying back and forth over the pits. He used a heliograph
only Scouts would notice, sun flashing off the plane's windows. We
wrote each series of flashes down in Morse Code, but couldn't cipher
it. We showed it to a soldier home on leave, but he couldn't break the
code either.

Blackouts were best. Sirens would go off, house lights blink yellow
to black window by window. From the front steps we watched night
blot out the streetlights block by block until the whole town was
unmade. We'd walk around the house with red cloth rubber-banded
over flashlights. Air raid wardens appeared from the dark to inspect

WITH MOUTHS OPEN WIDE

and complain about the guy up the block who didn't pull his shades. We'd sit in the living room and listen to the radio, kids dashing to the window now and then to peel back curtains and imagine searchlights tunneling the sky, hoping for bombers, wondering if this would be the time, until the All-Clear sounded. I learned something in Blackouts. I didn't know what, but I knew it was bigger than our house. Think of it: a power so strong it could make parents sit in the dark.

Captain Tom

The Mine Captains were tough sons of bitches who arrived knowing what Jehovah knew. They wore Cornish names like Nichols and Pengilly, Cohoe and Quick, and they were always by God called Captain. Tom Caddy made Captain in the iron mines of Michigan, and on the Mesabi he was Captain of the Penobscot and Susquehanna Mines in this new world where the Cornish faces turned iron red. He drove the first shaft into what would become the largest mine in the world.

The Captain was the bearing the mine spun on. He set pay by the foot and pay by the ton. He spoke flat to the miners, direct to the Superintendent, and up to no living man. Underground he talked slicing and stopes, drifts and tonnage and timbering, and at home he was silent or he proclaimed.

The Captain was called Tom only by his cronies. They liked to hunt. In Cornwall, the miners poached hares. On the new Mesabi, they hunted in buckskins and ate venison much of the year. Bloody this, bloody that, and Jesus H. bloody Christ. Once one of the dog pack groveled too much when blamed. Tom said, Why can't the damned dog be a man about it? None of them would ever swear in the presence of a woman.

Tom sought out a woman who agreed to be meek. She called him Captain, and ran him from that deference. Great-grandma Ellen was doilies and tea and a steely uncaring for all outside the blood. His father had married the same woman, his son would marry the same. After four or six or twelve children—do you count the dead?—in as many years, each of these deferent powerful women decided to sleep the rest of her life alone.

Submariners

Most of the gas-ration stamps go for family obligation, so all of them pile into the Ford on Sundays, off to Grandma and Grandpa's. At the end of the trip, just before Nashwauk, there is a long curve where, rounding it, the school bell tower comes into sight in the distance, high above the straight-edge horizon of the mine dump. When they see it, the man and kids play war movie, cry Submarine! and Up periscope! and become the Ford's crew, crying Fire one! Fire two! After firing, they chant seconds out loud, and the kids make explosions in their throats when the torpedoes reach the tower.

The Ford is rocked by depth charges, the man lurching the car back and forth with the wheel to evade them. As they drive closer, the bell tower slowly, elegantly as a doomed passenger liner, sinks toward the surface, and they watch batebreath as the tip of the bow finally slips below the horizon, and cheer. Just as the Ford dives under the railroad bridge and plunges into the sea that took the tower, they are in town. They are all below the surface now, suddenly quiet, tubes empty, hoping against depth charges.

After the afternoon and the women's faltering visit talk, the kids trying to stay busy and out of the way, and everyone pretending it is air they are in and not this family-thick amnion, after repeated bubbles of Fifteen two! and Go Godammit! exploding above the cribbage board where the red-faced officers contest, they all drive off into the dark. When they pass under the bridge, they do not drop ballast to rise dripping but safe again into moonlight, but stay submerged on the seafloor, hull breached, the crew separately encased in whatever breathing apparatus each can invent, periscopes down, silent running for home.

The Faces of Ancestors

The boy dreams again he runs through the lightless drifts and stopes of
an underground mine, face and shoulders tensed against repeated blows
he cannot prepare for. Ahead and behind, his grandfathers and great-
grandfathers wait to ambush him. When light blazes in the dream, the
cut rock turns mirror and fills with faces. He runs.

These old Cornishmen, underground for life,
whose faces learned to be the fractured
rock they spent their bodies to break, iron against
raw stone, this bore and blast and shovel
which turned faces bleak as the winter Atlantic
breaking the Cornwall coast.

In the mines there were no faces of wives
who would not forgive this ambush of their sons,
no faces of the scared boy except the one
held inside, the one forced to watch
his sons and son's sons driven inside,
generation after generation, the light
of each face snuffed as the child is
gagged and thrust into the hole.

Family and the narrow house
was a place to leave, to step into the shaft
and climb the long ladders down to the workings,
to slog down tunnels of night
in a clump of hard pale faces, the dark
pressing in on the head's candle,
to mine, to beat on rock and hope
the muscle would wear enough that
a man could go safely home, that his face
could mirror stone, the ore absorb enough of his gall.

The Changelings

He huddles in the pantry at Grandma's,
finger tracing the embossed mermaid
on the leather cover, eyes locked
in Hans Christian's tale. He reads
to leave the linoleum where once
he was content with clothespins.

He knows if he is any more here
today with these people who claim
blood relations, who will not confess
they stole him, the cold will grow
and the man will stop the car
to cut a switch tonight.

So for this time, he enters the mermaid.
He finds her love confusing, her strange
wish to leave the sea and walk
on stumping legs. To be away, apart,
to flow the green sea and watch
the human from distance, this he grasps,
but her wish, her love, slips through him.

But when it is time for her cruel proof,
his feet curl to the knives in her raw soles
and his legs draw up in her white agony.
He is amazed that some other knows, has
known this pretending to human,
changelings together from an element
other than this, fishes gulping fire,
unable to scream, unable to return.

Home Movies

As the camera pans, the people at the lawn party mug and work exaggerated words with silent mouths. They are all grownups in Kenny's black and white summer backyard, all dressed-up and drinking. Kenny and the boy watch a home movie in the basement. There is no sound. Kenny's mother is in the center of the screen now. She looks like laughter as she drains her glass and throws it over her shoulder. She puts her knees together and smoothes her party dress all up and down with her hands, smiling at the camera, tossing her hair. She has black lipstick and a white face. She reaches down to her hem and begins to lift. The picture wobbles on the screen. She slowly raises her dress to the tops of her stockings, lets go. The people in back clap silently, Kenny and the boy intent in the dark. The picture jerks. She reaches way up under her dress with both hands, doing something the boy can't figure. Making faces like an actress, she slowly pulls her panties down under her dress, steps out of them—one foot, stumbles, other foot—waves them gaily over her head. The other men and women clap and wide their mouths and show teeth. The screen goes white. While it rewinds the boy asks Kenny why she took off her pants. Kenny doesn't know. The boy wonders why Kenny showed him, but he doesn't ask. He wants to see it again.

The next day they sneak down the basement of Kenny's dad's department store to look at naked dummies. The boy is excited and scared, going down the back stairs, ready for the opened mystery. But when he sees the dummy breasts, they are just round things with no red in the middle. When Kenny slowly lifts one dummy's dress up, announcing like a circus man, the hidden part is just a blank smooth nothing. The boy gets mad. At first Kenny laughs, but he gets mad too, and throws open a storeroom door. The room is filled with a tumble of pink body parts, legs and arms, heads and middles all confused, men's parts and women's parts tangled, nothing between their legs, faces smiling dazed.

When the boy imagines first love years after, the dummies will return in dream, but the willing girl he undresses owns only the smooth blank. When the boy sees it he jumps up the department store stairs and out the alley door into the silent lawn party, people miming words and showing teeth. The woman begins to lift her dress. The boy knows she will be blank there, and is frantic to shut the projector off.

Yellowjackets

Wearing eyes of light as only
brand new creatures wear, Buck
clumsies through brush back of the cabin,
picking up burrs in his thick puppy fur,
and bumbles into a yellowjacket nest
in jackpine slash. They whirl into him,
burrow through fur to his skin and whine
his nose yellow as he howls blind—the boy
frantic with the pup's pain, beating them off.

The boy stands in the lake, holding
Buck's nose above water, trying to drown
the hornets, not feeling his own stings.
He digs fingers through fur for the buried ones
as they sting over and over, pulls them out
one by one and crushes them.

Wrapped in a towel, the pup shivers
in spasms from the poison, eyes
dull and staring, the boy unable to help
and unable not to feel. Shivering,
he connects with the woman's stunned look,
her incomprehension. He wonders
what her eyes were like before.

The Canterville Ghost

The boy sweats awake, dreamed wet again
by *The Canterville Ghost,* those first scenes
where the Black Knight charges terribly
with his lance leveled, and Charles Laughton
turns coward and quails, whips his horse
to his father's manor and hides in a pantry
off the kitchen, where he tries to not
breathe as the searchers arrive, the noble
men who would see honor done, listens again
as his stony father denies both knowledge
and possibility of his son's act. *Surely, then,*
the men say, *the lord could have no objection*
to our walling up the pantry?
The listener's panic catches *it would*
in his breath *settle matters, would it not?*
And satisfy honor. And again it's the dreamer
who will be buried alive, who watches
with horror but not surprise as the last brick
is mortared, who keeps silence until
the brick approaches the hole, the dreamer who
breaks screams *"Father!"* and wakes wet as
the brick is set in while the man refuses, for honor,
to hear, and continues fictions with his guests
as the mortar and the boy's throat dry.

He doesn't dream the rest: the ghost of the son,
doomed to haunt manor and descendants until
redeemed by Margaret O'Brien and billeted G.I.'s.
The father has kept the code. Terror
makes the dream, not betrayals. The boy
can anguish those, but never feel surprise.

He falls back into the closed-loop movie
dream, the word *Father* a way of making
ghosts, transparent sons begging to be heard,
fathers unable, for honor, to hear.

The Beating

The boy is dreaming in the dark
of a metronomic sound that punctuates
the night with glares of sullen red.
It is, slow and strong, the sound of one hand
slapping some boundary of meat.

Above this rise two muffled voices intertwined
like the bindweed on the corn.
Their words are slurred and full of teeth.
The dark voice chants of heat and rage,
the woman's winds around it a bewildered sodden begging.

The boy starts up, and stares,
and calms himself. In the dark
he gets up and shuts the open closet door.

Snow Forts

The boy has seen abandoned
Antarctic camps in Geographic
photos made years later by other
expeditions. Thick ice coats
everything, here a wall collapsed
from the growing pressure,
a chair overturned, there
a preserved table setting, unmoved
cup on the saucer. Even
the lightbulbs are rimed with ice.

The man has not spoken for days.
When his hand turns the doorknob
the long night begins again.
At table no one more than glances
from the plate. He makes
no requests, sits, drinks whiskey
on the rocks, expects to be served,
his cold pressure a glacier
obliterating all in expert slow motion.

The boy crawls through the tunnel
of his snow fort to the alabaster
chamber at the end, the round secret
place, and sits enclosed in walls
of white cold, winter light sifting through
the roof, sits safe, practicing white.

Mine Town: *Trick or Treat*

One of the little Carlson boys plays at his Grandma's and bored, rummages in her dresser, which he is not to do. Finds funny white robes packed with sachets in the bottom of one drawer, pulls them out. There are two, huge with separate pointy heads, big eyeholes sewn with tiny neat stitches. Sorcerer's robes, costumes for grownups, magic—imagines them at the Halloween party. Exciting new pictures of Grandpa and Gram.

He puts a head on. It blinds him until he adjusts the eyes. They'd have to take them off to bob for apples. The hoods would be perfect, though, for pin the tail. When Grandma surprises him like that she says *Jesus!* and yells, swats him on the bottom and says to never go in her drawers again! He looks later—the robes are gone.

When he thinks of it next he is thirty, says *Jesus Christ!* and can't quite imagine Grandma and Grandpa at the party.

The Tentative

The man is speaking to the boy,
who is wanting, who is wary.
His voice reminds the boy
of another time this happened,
when the voice was dark and warm

as the lake that summer night
they looked into the water
from the end of the dock.
They talked.
Their bloods fluttered

like the fringed lips of clams until
the taste in their mouths of
other who was self
and panic slammed them shut.
When he blurred his eyes
the netted stars were caught.
Nothing came of it.

He looks up at the man, lip
hardens on one, then both.
They withdraw once more
into their solitary skins.

Learning Ketchup

Dinnertime, digestion dependent on the man's
forbearance, the woman ready to be accepted
or be flayed, children wan and seated,
the formal requirements of Table.

The boy sits nearest the man, in his reach.

Tonight, meatloaf and potatoes, creamed
corn, homemade bread, lettuce, dills,
the ketchup bottle, tall and narrow-necked.

Table is the place for all to learn eating
from the man, who never grasps how
they can be so blind to his correction.

!—The boy hammers the end of the bottle again, no
ketchup, !— hammers, no ketch—the man abruptly
snatches it away, shows him How, rapping
the bottle neck against the edge of his hand.
It doesn't work. Doesn't work. Doesn't! The man
lifts the stubborn open end to his eye, stares it

down while a quirky deathwish in the boy's arm
bypasses his brain and calmly reaches across plates and
openhanded almost nonchalantly pops the bottle bottom.

Table frozen, forks halfway to mouths—a sudden red
gluts the man's right eye. The boy will die. Knows it,

can't believe—but cannot hold his laugh, the woman
squeezes her mouth but explodes, brother, sister
all rocking, rocking, and finally the red-eyed man himself
cannot but laugh and laugh, the boy unbelievably alive,

the man for once himself the fool, for once seeing red
    and laughing.

The Conspirators

With a gun. A knife. With a car.
Tip the canoe. Bury him alive—
Up to the neck and cut out his tongue!
In whispers they dare from bed to bed
as the shouts and slaps rain on,
whispers in darkness, considering ways.
They are matter of fact, but the boy
is astonished and warmed
that big brother would share
such a private unspeakable dream.
Cut off his eyelids, stake him out.
In the sun! Tie him tight.
They have never been closer.
Pour boiling lead in his ear.
It is night's center, the fantasy root,
each method cupped long in the mind
and offered in whispers,
each rasp of the throat
more grotesque and headier wine.
Lure him to quicksand—
Like the Mummy!
and watch as his fist disappears.
Do it together with hatchets.
Throw him off the edge of the pit.
They plot on in the dark in whispers—

Just get him so mad he burns up!
—that break into giggles. They have never
been closer, such brothers, so warm,
while downstairs the blows rain on.

Red Maples

It is just that he wants to give the woman
some autumn leaves for the mantelpiece,
for the fall of things, as the family leaves
the cabin to head back to weekday town,

and it's his search for the perfect
that has led him so far, always
just over there a patch of brighter maples,
a more excellent shape,

and when he does find them—reds to weep for
in perfect sprays—his jackknife
slips in their cutting and slashes.
In the instant before the wound bleeds
he sees into his wrist—meat, yellowfat, cut
veins, then the red welling

panics, flings the knife, keeps the leaves
unknowing, bashing through the dapplesun
woods unsure of the road, yellow
aspen swirling to his knees until
the Ford brakes and everyone mad
and his hand red as the leaves it holds,
the other squeezing the cut wrist.

So he stands on the green between
gravel ruts in front of the car
watching the man yell through the windshield

about where the hell he's been, what the hell's
wrong with him, blood spotting the leaves
as he stands to his dressing down.

He says nothing but walks to the woman's
window, holds out the maples
in his glued wrists and her afraid to
take them, rolling down the glass
then *O God he's bleeding*

and the boy slowly aware that the sprays are
more and more wet with blood
stands there trying to give the ruined leaves
to the woman, for the falling of things.

Scissor Man

Three darks of him gleamed when they caught light:
the handsmooth oak of his grinding wheel frame,
an eye from deep under his hat, the old bronze of his bell.
We followed him. He was mystery, the stranger from outside.

Once every Spring we heard his hand bell far away,
and blocks down the sidewalk under the elms
he would appear, a bent squiggle of dark.
Kids would holler *Scissor Man,* and gather in clumps
to watch him trudge closer under his load.

He never spoke to kids, never looked at us.
He wore all black under his wide brimmed leather hat,
a leather pad between his pack frame and bent back.
A sandstone wheel in a tripod of wood rode him high,
swayed with ditty bags lumpy with hints.

He never tried to get kids to like him.
I liked him for that. Once a year we heard him cry
Scissor Man, Scissor Man, knives and scissors, Scissor Man
and lift his arm and ring the bell again.

He touched his hat to housewives
as he set up his rig to sharpen. It had a folding seat
and a foot-treadle drive. While he ground knives
by someone's back door, we'd make a scuffing cluster
on the sidewalk, watching. When he was done
we followed him. It had always been this way.

Once a kid ran out in front of him to jeer, dancing back—
the Scissor Man stopped and studied him.
The kid's mouth closed, his feet froze. Those eyes
gleamed out at him from under the hat, but the Scissor Man's
mouth didn't move. Then his left hand sketched a sign,
and the kid ran home silent and wouldn't answer. That was lore.

We'd walk till we were too far from home, and watch him
shrink down the sidewalk under the elms, the bell
lasting longer than the eye. He never did talk.
I never heard him say a word beyond *Scissor Man, Scissor Man,*
knives and scissors, Scissor Man. He was *outside,*
the stranger in black. He gleamed. Sharpened. I followed him.

Fluency

Miss Prusha's oak yardstick would suddenly thwack! my left hand across three rows of desks. Our penmanship teacher hated the left and loved the right and true, which was named The Palmer Method. So she made me curl my left hand above the line I wrote on, and slant the endless exercise lines and ovals to the right, so I could at least approximate beauty. I did not.

In second grade she told me what "left" meant in Latin and French, and claimed that some countries exposed their left-handed children to the winter.

Refusing to be right, I curled my wrist and dipped cheap nibs into inkwells, my stubborn hand smearing each line as I wrote down the page. All through grade school, clouded blue papers, the words blearing in darker blue, a blue tattoo on my left hand's heel that I hid in my pocket like a brand that said *sinister* and *gauche*.

For a time, I wasn't left-handed. Except for writing and eating, I decided, I was ambidextrous: I could switch-hit in baseball and hockey, I could throw right-handed. Not well, but dexterously.

Toward the end of grade school, I found redemption and ended my shame. A passage rite of northern boys happens at night near a streetlight after a fresh snow, when the snowbanks and lawns beckon to be adorned. It was less a contest than a group celebration. We each staked out a pristine patch of white, exposed ourselves to winter and peed our names into it. My first efforts were jeered. But I was ambidextrous, I told myself, and was inspired to use both hands. Oh, my name was suddenly lovely, sweeping Palmer Method loops and curves and lovely round O's, peed two-handed into snow. Fluency at last!

My Method became the style that winter on the Southside. No beckoning snow was safe from our night fluencies. And no boy among us admitted there wasn't quite enough room for two hands.

The Marriage of Salamanders

He is not to move.
The old fraternity paddle cracks
on his skinned-down buttocks again and again.
The boy has come to know
he can welcome this burning.
It is his familiar, which has grown
into a power.
He will not cry out, not weep, will not react.
Heat can be hoarded and used.
The man's arm trembles in what he thinks of as
restraint, and cracks down again.
The boy's eyes are on the aquarium between the beds
where two spotted newts struggle
to mate, the male's arms
locked around the female's neck, his belly
stretched along her back, his hind legs squeezed
around her bulging abdomen.
She is larger, but
twist and convulse as she may, she cannot dislodge him.
They thrash together
in the green weeds and ooze, then sink
slowly, until another lashing of her tail

shoves them toward the surface again.
She is trying to get to air.
A wide bubble forms as she arches her neck and opens
her mouth, and the male tightens his grip.
The bubble escapes. They sink.
The boy cannot look away.
He is not to move.
It would break all rules.

Passage Rite

They call them Wet and Dry,
two abandoned pits concealed in woods and hills
south of town, hard enough to get to,
far enough to be worthy for a rite.
The path ducks through tilted concrete piers
and the huge rusted bones of mining machines.

Two dug holes a hundred yards across and deep,
exhausted of iron and long left to boys, between them
only a bridge of land at its widest the width
of outstretched ten year old hands.

Wet is a giant's version of that Mayan sacrifice well,
quarried red walls leading the eye down
to water cold and paintrock red and calm,
without a ledge to crawl out on.
Where a kid was supposed to have drowned.

And Dry, a mountain cirque closed off,
cliffed and gullied, steep fans of taconite scree,
bits of moss green scattered down the sides
where groundwater seeps, and on the floor
the thread of a stream, a clump of alder scrub.
As deep, but a somehow more attractive fall.

So the boy comes to the ritual bridge,
as all the Southside boys do in their time,

to try the narrow rock and gravel path.
Small rockslides down the widening sides,
and all muscles taut across and back.

He walks barefoot and he walks alone,
without touching fingers to the ground.
A few bad places where he wants hands and knees,
where a loose pebble or a sudden wish
can make him choose between Wet and Dry.

He knows nothing of why. The ancient choice
is dared, and he learns the passage of Wet and Dry,
learns more than the fear his flesh sings.
Somewhere on that sliding edge he finds
the wish to be undone, that wish as soon erased
as he gains the trees and waiting hands.

The boy does not know he will walk that narrow path
for years. Each time he does not belong
he will hear the falling rocks behind his feet,
and inch across the night between two ways to die.

Finding the Snake

The second night Dinty Moore Stew
bubbled in the can on a rock while
something leaped in and out of firelight,
a mouse with grasshopper legs—then
flicked once, twice over the coals
and jittered into dark. Riddles
in night eyes. Everything gets caught.

After we pitched the tent we sculpted
beach, became godkings who
carved new kingdoms out of sand.
Argued rules for conquest and naming.

The first night strangeness scraped
the tentskin. What giggled
in the pines fled from what crashed
while we tried to imagine sunrise,
sleeping bags unzipped.

The second day we skinnydipped, a first,
snapped Brownie Hawkeye photos. I have one:
thin Jerry in water to his knees, a trimmed
birch sapling held upright between his legs.
Taut muscles of boys. Patchy first hair.

One day we wrestled and neither would give.
It hurt. The fourth day we explored the lake's

pathless circle. We swore loud and laughed,
climbed trunks and sucked sneakers out of mud.

I caught a big garter snake, all quick silent
straining. Jerry carried it the rest of the way,
head thrusting again and again out of his hands
never not trying to escape. I told him to let it go.
Shouts, and Jerry walked ahead, jaw a knot.

He carried the snake to camp and
threw it on the sand, raised the sapling
over his head and smashed it
down on the stunned spine. And again.

Together we watched the snake writhe from
the head halfway back. It kept yawning
and biting its dead part. I slid the sapling under
and carried it outstretched to the dock's end,
slung it into clear water. Kept silence.

Later I looked. The snake was out there
in five feet of water, alive, chained
to the sand by his broken half, upper half
silently weaving the water. Something old.

The lake became impossible. Couldn't swim,
strained water from the creek.
We did not speak, but separately

With Mouths Open Wide

battered into waste the lands we'd carved.
When it came time to eat or sleep we shouted
blind. Slept rigid. Didn't touch.

Saturday we sat on our packs miles apart.
When the Ford rocked down the gravel to get us,
couldn't talk. My mother asked why.
We just loaded up and rode, one in front, one back.

Things refuse to die. Silence is the most
implacable. Every time I had to look it was still
weaving still aching for air refusing to drown.
I stopped walking out there to see. Knowing
is all backward. We get caught.

Art Disguised

As she emerges curve by curve from our fingertips and palms, she becomes the mystery we must complete. Her breasts are handpatted cones, made after the torso and plunked on top. Cousin Bob and I create from empty beach the woman we have begun to dream. She lies on her back. Our hands shape better than we know, her lines as strong in the sun as in vision, and she is ours. Where her thighs meet we leave for last, for we don't know what to do. We simply poke a hole.

We know our parents, up the path to the cabin, will misunderstand. This sculpting is both art and necessity. But we could be hauled away by our ears.

So we make a plan for camouflage. We pat up a whole slew of extra breasts, lined up off her right shoulder in a row, near the water where the sand will stay damp. Next to the breasts, we stick upright in the sand a row of white pine needle clusters. Stockpile sand in long mounds along her arms and legs.

It works like this: if we hear a voice, Bob will push the sandpiles in to obscure her body lines. I will quickly plop all the extra breasts on her chest and belly, stick the pine clusters here and there among the new huts, and Presto! A South Sea Island village. The parent will ask, *What is it?*

The natives, we will say, worship this large fallen head north of the village. Here, we will say, is a long narrow lagoon for their war canoes. And see here, at the end, the secret cave entrance, so the natives can avoid the climb up this steep hill to get to their huts.

We don't have to use it. Little Cousin Petey, mad because we won't let him help or even stick around and look, stamps her back into beach while the sculptors eat lunch at the cabin. He knows we can't tell.

Extensions

They must be close.
This is the man's imperative,
The boy's.
Neither of them know this to be true.
They would both recoil and bark
A laugh if it were said.

They hate each other.
The man does not put this in words.
The boy hums with it at night.
Both know this to be true.
It is not, it is a lie.

To caress the boy is to caress himself.
To caress the man is to caress himself.
Self cannot deserve it.
Impossible. But

They must be close, be
Intimate.
To touch is imperative.
To caress, impossible.
To hit is not.
They strike each other furiously.
Touch is touch.
They are close.

The Mummy

Some black odd-shaped thing he can't resolve, something with hair:
he slides down to it but the air yawns like a vast mouth and he
wants to leap backwards up onto the tracks. Crabs closer: the
front half of a dog, tight curled fur. The dog ends just behind the
ribcage, chopped off straight. It is dried, the fur cindered and dusty,
the nose varnished. The lips snarl back from the teeth, the mouth
opens to the dried black apricot of tongue.

He's seen his share of gutted deer, smelled the hot copper. It isn't
the death,but the halving, the mummy hollow as a broken drum.
No smell. Whatever rose from him is done.

He picks up a stick to prod it, throws it down. Climbs to the tracks,
scrambles down the other side and finds the hindquarters, legs
fixed in a trot, the loins collapsed in front of the hips. Town seems
a long ways off.

He climbs back to the tracks, leery. Tries to see his body sliced,
can't. Imagines the dog's headhalf falling down the bank, legs
scrabbling, mouth open in surprise, the track trembling in the
passage of the freight till all that's left is a dying rumble. When he
meets his friends at the beach, he says nothing.

But that summer over and over he pokes along these tracks to the
beach, watching air wobble above the rails, suit jammed under belt,
towel shoulder flung, never sure he's going to look. When he slides

down cinders and comes to rest dusting the headhalf, something slides down with him that he can't name. The mummy never changes.

There are three ways to the beach: the streets that little kids use, the south tracks with the mummy, and the trestle way. He starts in August to walk the tracks to the trestle that cuts the north end of the lake. On the trestle way, the railroad bed falls suddenly away and he is twelve feet above black water dotted with pilings, stepping from tie to tie over gulps of light. It does something strange to the soles of his feet.

If a train comes, he tells himself, his feet will hear it in plenty of time to outrun it, or to jump in and be all right, if he doesn't land on a drowned piling. He could hang by his hands from the beams while the locomotive tried to shudder him off. Likes that picture.

He takes the trestle way now for what's left of the summer. Never returns to the mummy. He doesn't think about why he is using the trestle way. He just knows it's time.

The Tales of Hoffmann

When the gondola crosses the screen
with the courtesan poised in the bow
and the boy first hears Offenbach's
Barcarolle, tears leap into him
where he sits in the darkened Granada
theater with a friend, and remain.
He has never heard so much.
After the movie they are expelled
into the downtown lights, where
he has a hard time concealing,
but so does Willy.
They do not look at each other or
anyone until they walk in
the dark between streetlights.
In the reflections of snowbanks
they begin to hum, still
not looking at the other's face.
But by the time they reach Sixth Street
they are glancing at each other's eyes
as they wordlessly sing the *Barcarolle*
over and over, and they sing it
under the streetlight, kicking holes

into a packed snowbank until their ears
crack with the cold, and they sing it
as they turn toward their houses
on opposite ends of Seventh, and hear
each other singing it for a block,
ringing it off the long arch of elms.
When they meet in the hall
the next day at school, they are shy.

The Gyrfalcon

White bird on white
snow with a small red fur in one
lifted feathered-to-the-talons foot,
a hooked beak of black.

I watch its eye: a deep returning.
But this black gleam, catching mine,
finds me simply here, now. Nothing
more. It gathers in and leaps.

When it cries I know my own
voice although I have never
heard myself. I leap at
what I carry inside, how simple
and fierce and welcome it is, the cry

welling up out of me in union
with this white austere
mystery beating now
in my ears and eyes and beating
in my mind a white
flame against the dark.

Here is every graced cold thing:
snow, pine green, shadowed
feathertrack, talon black,
sweptback wing, blue distant sky.

The Color of Mesabi Bones

2

He tries to find the white bird in words,
makes something like a creed:

> *White and clean and does not care,*
> *Black and fierce and does not need.*
> *Not caring keeps it pure.*
> *Not needing keeps it free.*

He says it before the nightly order of dinner,
says it during a beating, he says it
in the morning dark, deliver newspapers.

No one else has seen it. He doesn't know how
it could have a name, it is vision not
words. But he begins to doubt as he learned
to doubt that he could fly, the time
he pedaled calmly off the roof
without a bike because he'd dreamed it so.

Months later he finds it at the library, in
a color plate of raptors: **Gyrfalcon**, king
of falcons, that like ermine, only
ancient kinds could carry on their arms.
According to the book, not found here.

He knows more. Gyrfalcon is in him,
too much to contain, yet he knows now
he has found what he must hold, or try,
that this white and beaked uncaring
is both what and for.

The Invisible Boy

Eyes, from that ceiling corner of his bedroom. From just beyond sight, over any shoulder. Whenever alone, the Watchers watch. Walking to school. From the bedroom window. Sometimes the boy forgets. A sudden start returns them. On the dawn paper route, from every shuttered window, curtains stirring. In the classroom. The Watchers. At the Newsette, sneaking looks at Argosy or Police Gazette. He never asks about it as he moves through time. Who would there be to ask? He assumes everyone has them.

So he becomes the Watcher of himself. Sees how he must look, how each move must look, learns the empty face, the falsely full. But he discovers a rule: If on his bed he reads and becomes other, he turns invisible. Even to the ceiling corner. But he fears the times his own eye flutters into sleep or any natural moment.

The Watchers are everywhere except—the second rule—the woods. There are other watchers there who scare the first away, the wild eyes he doesn't mind. Woods eyes can make fear, but they don't aim it. This fear is clean. In the woods he is visible even when he forgets himself.

But in town he must watch himself, so in the Watchers' watching he will not be discovered. He learns to wrap himself in semblance, as Claude Rains wraps himself in long white surgical bandage, around and around the skull leaving only the hollow eyes. This is the part before he goes mad.

The boy watches and wraps so well he stands behind his windings and all think they are seeing truly. His wrapping makes friends, works, drinks, lindys at the Legion, acts in school plays, laughs, even kisses. And in time even he thinks the gauze is himself.

But after years dancing becomes impossible. He no longer can tell when the watcher is Them or self. He no longer knows that is a question. But something is. He begins to see his wrapped seeming as the way he stays invisible—or is it a display of love for his wounds?

Pictures sift for his new knowing: *Ancient linen wrappings tattered and stained . . . fog . . . the Mummy's wrist and clutching hand slowly disappear into quicksand.* Wrong reel.

Shots flatten the night as he leaps through glass. As he dies, the girl weeping, his flesh slowly returns to the visible, first the time-lapse skeleton, then the overlays of viscera, veins, muscle, the moment of eyes . . . No.

Use this one: *Shots flatten the night, and shouts. "Where'd he go?"* Cut to: *Himself unwrapping bandages in a mad transport, spinning them off and dancing down the moonlit road, the long white ribbons dragged and dangled and finally snagged on bushes and left. He heads for the woods, a whirling in leaves.*

Mine Town: *Knowing Where You're At*

He sees nation in every cheekbone, every movement of a lip. Pops Schibel stands in front of Palace Clothing, greeting all in their mother tongues. Sees nation in a walk, the way a scarf or babushka is worn, and knows which of his seven tongues to greet. He apprenticed in Helsinki and Riga, Malmö and St. Petersburg, and in none of them could he own land.

Pops knew all these sons and daughters of hardrock miners who drilled underground in Budapest and Helsinki, Cornwall and Wales before they came across in the 1880s and 90s, jostling sons and daughters of the Canuck and Swede loggers who stayed after the pines was cut, hustling the Chippewa, elbowing the steerage immigrants who came from Italy and Montenegro, Slovenia and Finland with notes on their clothes, all these Greeks and Irish and Poles, Baltic Jews, Chinese.

Nation is basic on the Mesabi. And where that tension rules, so must clarity. The glaring clarity that lets you know where you're at—like it or not. The restful clarity that saves the energy of *politesse*, saves work, allows work. Clarity sired by necessity out of Babel.

Here, even the Italians say Eye-talian. To the rest, Dagos. French Canucks are Frogs. Serbs and Slovenians and Bosnians all lump into Bohunks. Cornish are Cousin Jacks. Finns so lucid and sure they are simply *Suomilainens*, Finlanders. Necessity: second and third-generation kids routinely insult their friends to greet them, to defuse their parents' dislikes, their own suspicions. *Hey Dago, how ya doin'?* Insult with a smile, to enable love.

Years later in Anthropology 1A, I hear a lecture about the Eskimo custom of *joking relationships,* crude ritual insults to lower winter's tensions and prevent murder. I watch Norwegian and German farmboys furrow their brows and push forward heavily in their chairs, trying to comprehend, and for a change, I lean back and cross my feet, happy to hear of other civilized groups in the north, knowing where I'm at.

The Quest in This Season

The boy is looking for a tree.
His three pound axe is shoulder slung,
his legs are breaking trail through snow thigh deep.
Although he sweats, frost is crystal in his hair
and snowmelt trickles down between his scarf and neck.
His eyes are up and circling as he plows,
searching for a Christmas balsam to fill the green demand
his father placed, like perfection, in his eye.

The boy does not know, but stirring in his mind
is a picture held behind his eye for years,
from an picture book about a Christmas tree
who sought recognition, who to praise the Birth begged
to be severed from the root. In the story,
when the tree gets his wish and is cut,
God turns his needles into multicolored crystals
shining from inside. So much for roots.

It is well the boy knows little of his mind.
He is cold and stumbling wet and catching boots
on buried hazelbrush. He finds it hard to swallow.
Through fading light the snow hangs blue on boughs.
He believes he is searching for a Christmas tree.

School Maiden

       Edna Gay Schaaf, ancient
       and dour, cracks one of her
       canes across a desktop.
       For choral reading, she has us declaim
       World War One horror voices from the graves
       of Flanders' fields, offering to blood
       poppies but never forgetfulness.

       Between choruses, between
       the crack of canes, she continues
       her ritual recital of the time
       she shook hands with Teddy Roosevelt
       during the Bullmoose campaign . . .

       So purely impossible then
       to imagine her fresh and parasoled
       in a long white dress, a maiden's blush
       across that ravaged face.
       The ease of such vision now.
       To the Colonel ever faithful, but
       never forgetful of us, one of her canes
       always whistling through the air.

The Length of These Generations

My salty old Grandma, polka dots and net,
French Canuck and four foot eight,
who stretched those tiny loins five times for heads,
loose-boned, the whisker-rubbing miner's wife,
walking old that day at the zoo,

with my mother at five foot two, a tailored peach
who married the mining engineer,
walking middle-aged now at the zoo,
with my sister in pink at five foot seven plus heels,
who pushed a stroller through that Easter zoo.

Grandma caught the titters and crowdflow
where the zebras were, and saw the tumescent stallion,
she did a double take and cried out in her cackling old voice,
My God, girls! Isn't he hung!
The taller girls enclosed her quickly then,
and skins burning like Easter eggs hustled her away

to me, astonished and stumbling, who could not stop
laughing, and picked up that tiny old bawd
so rooted in sense, in earth, and danced her in a circle
while we both cackled until tears which spoke,
together this once, of some lovely freedom in age,
and some loss in the length of these generations.

Mine Town: *Uncle Joe at the Ballgame*

Beneath the concrete bleachers
of the Eveleth Hippodrome, lines of boys
in letter jackets routinely slouch both dies
of the corridors, wait for girls in their threes
and fours to come along, to
ricochet them with their hands
from boy to opposite boy, copping quick hard feels.
some girls swear, some grow quiet and scared,
some like it, and a few in leather,
like Cookie or Tincups, dare them: *You wanna
wake up with your balls in your mouth?*

Above the basketball tournament
semifinal game is suddenly stopped:
the PA crackles and announces simply *Joe*—
Joseph Stalin has died. Stalin is dead. The men
and women in the crowd surge upright and cheer
wild, throw deep sounds and shrill sounds
high into the Hippodrome while the kids
look around at them, unsure. The cold warriors
exchange smiling epithets with neighbors,
slap a few backs, sit back down.
The ref blows his whistle, tosses a kid the ball.

A Party to Enormity

The boy twistfingers the flags on Gyp's legs,
iron-stained memories of chasing rabbits
through the ore dumps before he was hipshot and could run.

He was told it had to be, that Grandpa's last springer
must be put away, so after supper the man and boy
drive Gyp's nervous whine from Grandma's to the vet's,
without voice, the boy not sure why he was along—
to quiet the dog, he guessed.
It was not their habit to share.

Now and then one of them pats Gyp's head
saying *There, boy* or *Hey, old timer*
and it comes off awkward, like something badly rehearsed,
like the hint of lie in every Norman Rockwell illustration.

As they enter all of them recoil from the flaring
veterinary smell, from the air-hung pheromones
that burn terror into old Gyp's nose.
The man says simply *I can't stay here*
and walks into the night.

The boy lifts Gyp to the porcelain table
where dog claws skate forever into fear
while Doc fills a hypodermic from a bottle of emerald green.
The boy hugholds the dog, calms him, strokes him,
feeling on his palms the ulcers on that trembling neck,
wipes the mattered spaniel eyes.

Doc shaves the center of the left front paw
to expose the vein, squeezes it up, inserts the needle
and simply shoves, and before the needle is down an inch
the boy feels through the chest one brief jerk
and then cessation, and he is holding
nothing to his breathcaught ribs.

The old vet confides to the empty boy
that he keeps in his dresser next to his bed
a hypo of this crossboned green in case the crab
finds its way into his gut, and reminds the boy
that he can now lay down the limpness he is holding in his arms.
The boy thinks, through the dry center of a tear,
that beds are not clawmarked porcelain.

In this moment's emptiness the boy
loses all the space inside where Bambi lives
and Old Mother Westwind whirls away.
No room left for notions of a Gyp made young again,
chestblaze flashing, prancing up to some celestial hunter
with an eternal mallard in his mouth.
So he goes outside to see to the man, wondering
what will happen to the cooling meat that's left.

Outside the man stares into the dark.
He speaks no word of comfort to himself or to the boy

for fear of what will leap out from his voice,
that there would break from him his father's grief
for this last dog, his mind wandering
in the tubes and drains they'd broken Grandpa with.
Abandoned, he founders in his taconite gut.
The boy stands a few feet away,
and they share only the muteness of dogs.

Permission

The boy is in the green
urgency of light which spills
through terraced maple
leaves and falls to calm
the shadows moving on his face.
Sprawled on his back
in last year's leaves,
he is blinking, sap
has finally risen to
the corners of his eyes.

Bright shafts of green play
upon his body like sunlight falling
through clear water into
rippled sand. He
weeps, but cannot name
this easy welling
of the tears he will not use
for pain, until

he turns his head and
sees outside this light

which hollows him,
the tracery of veins the snails
have tongued from fallen leaves,
this blurred lace that nets
his shadows, and names
this welling *joy*.

All He Can Think Of

When he leaves, he will burn
across the world, skywriters
will name him in letters
a hundred feet tall, biologists
will speak of him in reverence,
his photo, pipe in hand, will gaze
at the reader from book jackets.
Or by choice he'll labor in obscurity,
the reward the great work itself.
He will have a fine life. A fine life.

It's these people who gnarl
him now, this place. Leave.
All this dreary damned red,
and the man's slung hands,
the woman's hopeless craving,
the mirror's secret mad faces
will fog, wobble around the edges
and in a triumph of waking
dissolve from his brain into time.
His eyes burn with it: Leave.

But when the moment
arrives, all he can think of

is a waxed wooden floor,
bars of afternoon light falling
through Venetian blinds
like a cello score, a velvet pillow
of green, a yellow windup tractor
whirring on its side, dustmotes
swirling in light above them
as if a throat had just cleared
or someone stood quickly
and walked from the room.

The Creature

Black and white. So much more
like life than Technicolor. Print it.
It never fades, never
loses its edge. Beneath
yet another broken castle
the Wolfman finds
a huge body dressed in black
frozen into white ice.
The deep face is never—
Lon Chaney, Jr. scrubs the ice
with his sleeves—is
never clear,
wavers in torchlight
in the refraction of ice,
never clear but we
know that face, know
who it always is
before he builds the fires
to thaw the Creature

who is not dead and will not die.
Mind scrubs at the ice, commits
horror again.
The Creature never fades, never
loses his edge. And I
build the black & white fires
over and over, and
melt him into life.

The Color of Mesabi Bones

In the Lone Jack mine in 1914
twenty three-men with shovels and picks
curse and choke in dust and pray
in a motley of tongues
when the underground caves in.
They stay, the Lone Jack ore for a marking stone,
their bones stained red with leaching iron.

Iron birthed red, torn from the earth,
and miners and towns took its
colors and ways, reds of dust and rust,
of fresh blood and dried, of SCAB
slashed in paint across a store, of Indians
who would not disappear, of the Klan's fires,
Wobblies, union bombings, socialist Finns—
the only unred the blacklist.

Cars red with oredust halfway up,
and in November the gutted deer tied to fenders
streak the dust with blood.
Where it pools on running boards, kids
dare each other to touch it.

Iron ore, iron oxides. Ocher, carmine, vermillion,
rust where the soft vein muddies the spring,

paintrock, stroked for centuries on cheekbones,
painted on the cliffs of Lac la Croix,
designs of another autumn, that vision lost.

Kids who live close to the open pits
mix paint from trackside dust
and for a game dip a finger
and mark their faces with their caste,
or smear the whole face, like Dad's.

The weathered basements of abandoned
company towns, houses taken off.
Hidden under tansy stalks in what
was yard, the red dust coats scattered stones
painted white once by a Finn miner's wife
to border the path now broken.

Working the underground drifts
in darkness and mud and carbide hiss,
in union suits, overalls, helmet and lamp,
rubber boots, pants and rubber coat,
and dripping from timbers through
five hundred feet of rock, water down the neck,
all stained the color of the Lone Jack bones.

Domestic reds: sinksuds, the bathtub ring,
the red rim of the drunken eye.
Red anything that stands to the wind—
house siding blown dirty pink, yet

the closer to the mines and tracks, the more
stubborn small white houses.
Red anything that runs or rolls on the ground—
no dogs are white. So much iron ore dust
you can't tell when a thing is rusting.

Coming off shift they all look alike,
Canucks and Bohunks, Dagos and Finns, all
the cold gritty red that won't wash off,
fingerwhorls, hands, fissured
necks like dendrites mapped in red,
and this is the color of the Lone Jack bones.

Pit descended, pit forgot, miners
crowd the counter of the Magic Bar,
red wide mouths barking slurs and laughs,
tired punchboards sagging like the thought
of the wife and kids in the VA house,
the lighted beersign waterfall
snared in cylinders of wet glass,
caught in drying rings below the faces.

The old men nodding, used to this,
watch the Wobblies pack the Range in the '16 strike,
riding the rails of empty ore trains,
watch them march, red flags and neckerchiefs,
watch boxcars of scabs unload
who can't talk English good either.

The Color of Mesabi Bones

Hanging on the edge of the closed Majorca pit,
the abandoned washing plant, the windcraze of loose
galvanized iron trembles and bangs, hollering time.

In sadly named Aurora,
the strikers tear up boardwalks
for barricades, and Elizabeth Gurley Flynn
climbs up on top, daring the company goons to fire,
a homely Delacroix heroine dancing on tinder.
So many shot dead this year,
buried far above the Lone Jack bones.

The mine dumps dwarf houses on the outskirts
of towns, foothills of gravel and rock dropped
first by glaciers, draglined and trucked
from the open pits. Above them brood
the worn granite breasts of the Giant's Range,
oldest earth, the blasting shaking even this.

The huge torch rallies of the Twenties
Klan, filling ballparks and picnic grounds,
the Jessie Lake encampment, couples
sparking in Model T's on the hills above
larking kids, mom and dad, grandpa and gram
in bedsheets, burning righteous
crosses across the Range, native
speakers all, or those who blended well,
shouting Catholics, kikes and anarchists!
Fire in the Lone Jack bones.

Iron ore. Hematite, from the Greek
haimatites, like blood, like what streamed
from the eyes of that old king, blood
of mother blindness, the vision lost.

Saturday night alleys behind the Legion dance,
the blood of smashed noses on white snow.
And every long winter's newspaper murder/suicide,
dried blood in a snowed-in cabin in the muskeg.

This dust, this red patina
on truck tires, shovels, coils of fuse,
draglines, timbers and railroad tracks,
this coating in throats and hawked handkerchiefs —

All night, locomotives full of steam
slowly huffing ton after ton of ore
up the steep tracks to the crushing plant, shuddering
and blowing off like horses at the top.

This drear overlay of rust
on tailings ponds and roadside weeds,
on sparrows taking dustbaths near the mine,
on the chain stretched across the company road —

And red is the color of bones.

Presences the Blood Learns Again
(1997)

The Cornish and the Gorse

If you grasp the gorse, or fall into the furze
and rake your skin, you take on Cornish character.
The Cornish and the gorse are either side of one green leaf.
They are synonyms, inseparable,
they swap their substance and their breaths.

Call it what you will, your fancy's choice,
when rich in bloom say golden gorse,
when plain greygreen say furze.
Both its names are coarse and carry spines,
long and maddening and fierce.

For long years of the backalong, poor Cornish women
carried boiler, clothes and brandis to the well
and gathered furze to build their fires.
Rinsed clothes were spread upon the furze to dry
while the women bit the spines from out their fingers.

Cornwall cannot be thought without the golden gorse.
For century heaped on century, children of the poor
who had no turves walked to landlords' hedge and
furze brake to gather stog and branch, fuel to heap on
upturned kettle to bake pasty, barley bread and pie.

For forever and for more, the Cornish and the gorse
have shared their very elements: oxygen held now
in leaf, exhaled, and now in blood,

carbon now in branch of gorse and now
in bones dug into churchyard soil.

The Cornish have from time unknown
laid their bones in earth to give the furze their fertile fire
to transform into branch and golden flower—
on sacred hearth the furze returned the fire it stored
and warmed the winter gales.

The furze brake always spreads and grows
across the Cornish moorlands
strung with menhir, ring and bones,
graced with bracken, heather bell and ling.

When the gorse explodes its seeds they spray out far
and scatter: at Blackheath there is a furze-shroud mound
where after the Rebellion, the Cornish dead were thrown,
the old bargain carried to the foreign east.
Atoms of those men still bloom.

When the gorse's seeds explode they scatter wide:
In the miners' diaspora, 300,000 Cornish
were offered to the soil around the globe.
Atoms that were once gorse lie
inside those miners' bones on every continent,
dreaming still, perhaps, of flowering in gold.

Bal Maid at the Ding Dong Mine

for Eliza Jane Hall, d. 1873

Across the valley from the Men an Tol, one hill over from the
Nine Maidens Stone Circle stands what's left of the Ding Dong
Mine, romantic now, machinery gone, a ruin, but the engine house
stands, the stone chimney still thrusts up. The mine was begun
when Romans camped here and ordered the Cornish to dig. Ding
Dong had a famous bell which called the workers out as dawn broke.
The men and boys over ten or twelve began their descent into dark
underground, women, girls and little boys and old men took up their
tools to dress ore. The women are bal maids, mine-maidens, long
white Hessian aprons pulled over dark Victorian dresses.

Eliza Jane isn't thinking about wheels or circles of any sort, except
maybe the endless round of her days, waking to that bell, cobbing ore,
walking home, fixing dinner and tomorrow's pasties for the men, who
arrive later, having had to climb to grass a thousand feet, then sleep
and then the morning bell again. No circles, except maybe a ring. She
thinks of meeting a man to marry. She gives her head a little shake to
waggle her earrings, and laughs. Alice Adams laughs back. The noon
bell tolls.

For the bal maids the shift is ten hours, receiving the ore from the
kibble, barrowing it to stamps, then sorting the ore from the till. Or
buddling the ore in cold water up to their calves. One break at midday.
Balmaids start work as young as six or eight years, as do the boys,
sorting ore for pennies, and work their way older.

Alice wants to wash at the stream; Eliza says no, wanders to the engine house and gazes up at the huge crown-gear wheel of the whim-winding engine. It looks almost a roundabout set on edge. It's idle now. She climbs up the wheel on impulse. From the stream, Alice shouts to her in a tizzy, so Eliza climbs down. Then the warning bell rings: the engine will engage and the wheel will turn. Eliza looks around her, clambers up on the wheel again while it begins to turn and cries, *I will go round!*

Bal maids dress the ore and dress themselves up to do this work. The older maids—women are "maids" whatever the age—wear the gook, a white headdress that covers their shoulders and head. Each parish has its own style. Some gooks have wings, like gulls about to take flight. Younger maids compete in jewelry, pendant earrings and showy necklaces of beads. They have no other life but Sunday and payday.

When the engine stops at Eliza's long scream, the whim driver runs out to see. Her clothes are caught in the cogs, and parts of her body. Alice runs up and wails Eliza's words, *She said 'I will go round!' like it was a roundabout she would ride!*

Sunday the sermon is on *willfulness in girls,* and how *rivalry in dress is becoming the order of the day, and thus are many led into temptation. Nothing is thought of but foolish display.* Eliza's funeral follows. When the Ding Dong Mine is closed years later, the famous bell goes on display in Madron Church.

Coming to Grass

Cornishman: a man at the bottom of a hole, singing.

They came to grass at the end of the day.
They climbed from the Dark to grass
and carried the Dark up with them.

After a long day of night with only
the head's candle for light,
after aching hours of sledging iron
against candle-gleamed borer,

grass was the surface they climbed to
through a thousand feet of Dark—
Over and over they pulled their weight up the rungs
as their hearts rang the rib cage,
to come up to light and grass-green,
but to carry Dark with them unseen.

Dark changed the strong men,
shortened their tempers, stubborned beliefs,
roughened their tongues—
Dark led them to think
they were the ones who could see.

But in the mine, on ladders, in chapel, in pub,
bearing this Dark is what taught them to sing.

Cornish Hedges

Thirty thousand miles of hedge
square off this land,
built hedge of moor stone,
old granite strewn once on Cornwall
like the jackstraws of stone gods.

A Cornish hedge, a proper hedge,
is two walls of stone sloping in
toward a planted top,
walls as far apart as they are tall,
and filled between by subsoil rab.
Most stones are roughly squared.

Consider these hard stones:
each lifted up by hands and thighs,
backs and sweat, set in place,
each slope wall fitted, built up apart,
rab pounded between them.

Consider two thousand years of back break:
at Zennor old hedges run in Stone Age curves,
from a time when life was round,
where fields still sound neolithic names.

Blackberries eaten from the hedge are sweet;
butterflies sip from them nectar.
Their coppiced trees gave withies for wattle

and a slower fuel than furze
to cook the barley bread.

Lay your hands on hedge stones,
feel the spirit and the sweat.
When you admire the tidy fields all hedged,
think millennia of strain and knuckles barked.

Twite in the Churchyard

The key word under the twite's picture in the bird guide is "fearless"

The stones lean one way
and the afternoon light another;
the gravestones choose their own
angles but all lean, slant sun cuts;
relief in their moss and streaks.
A small bird bounces about
the place upright, invites me to do
the same, straighten from my search
for names on weathered slate
to stretch my back and approach
this small bird restless in the cedar.

It allows me near without flying, and near.
I sway the space like a leaf, reach
out a hand to touch what will happen
and find a bird without fear.

It lets one finger stroke feathers
while its head cocks to look at me.
We agree the world is a curious place
if we can still touch, and that
this graveyard was in the Domesday Book
and has a right to lean,
but there is reason for us
restless brief lives to try to stay upright.

Center-post Stones at the Iron Age Village

The weight of lived lives
jolts when I touch
the center-post stones,
in this place people lived
for a thousand years
but left when the Romans went home.

Their eyes thought round:
the houses are circles,
the walls are circles of stone,
the holy well is just down the way.

I know the human moment
with my hand on the center-post stone.
Grass grows where floor stones once lay,
and light falls where the roof's shadow.

Here everything curves.
Small rooms off the main
curl away, the out-walls curve,
the boulders that make the walls,
all rounds to the circle
they lived in so long.
All that is left are grass-topped walls,
an apron outside of welcoming stones,
and at each house-circle's center,
the center-post stone,

a massive moorstone with a socket carved
deep and round, base for the tree trunk
to hold rafter and purlin and thatch.
It is here, when I touch, I see hands
hang a cradle, a candle—plait
leather, rough a child's dark hair,
rest a palm on smooth wood.
It is quiet; I can't quite find voice.
Grass grows where these hands lay,
and light falls where the shadow.

Men Gurta

The wind that blows between the worlds
cut through him like a knife.
—Kipling

There was never a stone better named
than Men Gurta, Stone of Waiting.
Menhir, longstone, great patient stander.

It waits on the high point of St. Breock Downs, moor
that's been moor for thousands of years, since people in skins
cleared the trees and raised the stone called Waiting.

The moorland's long been rock and peat and wet,
useless to men, except, being men, to defend,
too rocky for much to disturb the wait of Men Gurta.

Only on Midsummer Eve, when the fires are lit on
the high hills of Cornwall,
is the wait of Men Gurta disturbed.

Do stones measure time?
These fires have just begun.

It has stood here and waited four thousand years.
Men Gurta is blank, no carved words from a time-haunted age.
No stone could better be named.
Blank is the whole face of waiting.

Morning Earth: Field Notes in Poetry
(2003)

Morning Earth Online
(New Work)

From www.morning-earth.org

About My Morning Earth Online Poems

Morning Earth Online is first a celebration. *The poems rise out of brief daily experiences with nature that I accept as gifts—of joy, of laughter, of awe, of surprise, of learning. Writing these poems is a daily practice—if you will, a devotional practice—for me, a way of integrating my separate self with the whole.*

A number of the poems below are from my book Morning Earth: Field Notes in Poetry *(2003). They were originally written daily and sent via email to subscribers. The rest of the poems in this* Morning Earth *section are from www.morning-earth.org, my nonprofit organization's online presence, which emails daily poems to subscribers and offers resources in the confluence of art and ecology.*

After a crippling stroke some years ago, I was surprised and delighted to be alive, and found myself filled with a persistent mood of opening. I decided to dedicate myself to a celebration of earth life, in my art and in my teaching. The poems that follow are deliberately simple and transparent enough to be readily accessible.

The poems' intent, or their hope, is to help people reconnect with their intuitive love of the wild. Although we have put much earth life in peril, nature is far from dead. Happily, we are still part of the community of life from which our culture too often tries to divorce us. Take these little poems as proofs that the wild is still alive to sustain us, and still offers to the careful eye images that heal.

Tasting Other

Warm fall winds
rustle cattails, sigh grasses dry.
Sulfur butterflies lollop down fields,
let breeze take them, uncurl
tongues to taste red clovers,
asters, tall clovers white.

Paused foldwing, one sulfur
tumbles a golden primrose,
another sails from a clover head
and spots the first, then in flight
with delicate antenna just

strokes the first,
so both leap, fluster up
to quick-taste other, as quickly part
to catch the breeze away.

This quick dance bobs the paths of lives:
to taste the other before the cold,
so briskly wind does sweep us fluttering along.
The tasting makes the dance.

Seed Wind

A milkweed pod
flowers its silk onto the wind:
the pebble-skin yawns, white
billows from the center,
a gust looses floss, the first flight
of seeds ride their silks
already high and free,

off to feed caterpillars
and turn them into kings—

what the wind is for.

Solstice Sky

This long night solstice sky is filled with fires
that burn through air so cold
on this small northern place
of tilted Earth, air so cold
it carries echoes of the void,
the heatless absolute of space,

yet these ancient stars
are the memories of fires
that burned long before eyes
ever tilted up to them
and thought of light.

Feathered Ears

As sky begins to glow, a barred owl
sits a hoarfrost branch and looks around,
around, and all the other way around,
a pair of hungry eyes perched upon a swivel,
but mostly he is feathered ears:
he hears the tiny sounds
of mouse claws on the crystal snow
where tunnels end and day is risked for food.
Owl's hunt is so still that when I see a talon flex
I almost hear long hoarfrost crystals
break and sift to ground.

Life as Ice

In leaf litter under snow, the small
wood frog would gleam with ice
if sunlight glowed so deep.
His raccoon mask is fixed
and hard as painted stone,
for he has become both life and ice.
The eyes are closed, the mouth line
grins at the trick this frog has played
on the winter of the world,
for wake he will from cold
and hop bright-eyed through woods, slowed
at first but gleaming with a frog's fine living glow.

Flung

The snow has melted away
from where the doe had lain,
the doe a truck flung into drying cattails,
melted away from where
I watched her disappear last fall for days.

How strange:
she was whitetail doe, mother of fawns,
then with a truck's one quick blow
she was carcass, carrion for crows.

At autumn's end I saw still
her hair and bones, forelegs
and dark, polished hooves,
white skull, long spine.

And now the snow has gone
and with it every trace of doe.
Earth slowly melted her,
took her back to roots sure
as sun quickly warmed this snow,
and lifted it away.

Life Delights

Morning earth speaks sweet
everythings in my ears:
rattle of woodpecker, thin chickadee,
warble of the jay, hoarse muted trumpets
from distant geese,
two big barking dogs,
squirrel scold, dove coo,
the tick of tiny paws.
Sandbagged again, goosebumped,
I can only think of Blake:
For everything that lives is holy;
life delights in life.

Refuge

The rotting upright trunk is full of holes
the pileated woodpecker cut with his long beak,
holes carved wide and chiseled deep.
In the trunk I find a refuge, a hollowed place
where one small tough bird,
a chickadee or junco, put its back to winter wind
long winter night after winter night, leaving
droppings to tell the story now in spring.
It left one gray feather there.

This little refuge gives me one:
that the woodpecker in its need
saved a life it neither knows about nor cares;
we live together here, and at times
we help without trying
by Earth's design.

Suppose

Trees are suddenly on flower,
catkins dangle green and gold, oaks
blush red, plums white, all abrupt
as the blush and bloom of puberty.
What magics push through stems
these sudden blooms
and the greening ears of leaves?

Suppose it is spring choirs:
the primal nightsong of the frogs,
the firstlight chorus of the birds?
Say it's so.
Say the birds release the trees,
while frogsong greens plants close to soil,
old liverwort, mosses tossing spore caps,
berry bushes, lily thrust.

The choirs are fully throated now,
in these brief days when dawnbright birds
overlap the nightsong of the frogs,
and all turns green and flowering,
and children almost know their loveliness.

Sudden Ambiguity

A perfect morning mushroom
swells from roadside grass,
broad and domed, a stool
for royalty of toad.
Its color fawn,
its texture suede,
its temperature amphibian,
it is the autumn apple of earth's
hidden streams, soon ripe-ribbed
with spores below its parasol
now opened to the fine rain
that sent perfection swelling out of soil.

Leaf Light

Off the trail a yellow aspen leaf
spins on a spider silk
spins with the breeze
without sound
blinks light
winks bright
twice
each round

Inside Me Wild

The wood thrush pours morning into me
like early light through basswood leaves,
a song that glows me out of bed.

Then pileated woodpecker cries out
his ululating almost-laugh,
gives me goosebumps on my joy,
wakes inside me all the wild.

Glacial Speech

This land is what the glaciers spoke.
That hollow a vowel that took a century to gouge,
that lake uttered by a plunging waterfall,
this sandhill murmured by a stream
beneath a thousand feet of ice.

Glaciers spoke this land:
the slow grind of boulder teeth
growled simply, finally,

Ground.

Placenta

On a forest floor, go to your knees.
Cup your hands before you.
Move aside dead leaves.
Trowel your fingers into earth
and lift some cupped before you, close.
Let your nostrils open wide.
What you smell has always been,
is then, is now, is when.
What you hold is all alive.
Your seven senses know it.
Look closely. Deep.

Nets on nets of threads connecting all.
This is earth's placenta, this secret
densely woven lace that streams with life.
The threads are fungus roots which feed
each plant and tree upon this forest floor.
Each rootling of each plant expands by ten
embraced by microscopic fungus tubes
that weave a web of food that flows
two ways: the plant is fed
with rock dissolved and water;
the fungus root is fed with light
the plant transforms with
water, air, and rock dissolved.

Now replace the mother earth.
Her nets will heal. Your hands have held
the moving crucible of life, and if you tremble
well you should, for you are in it, of it,
living, here, where you will always be,
where you have always been.

Centering the Ripple

Ripples and reflections occupy spring waters,
occupy the depths among the willow roots.
Hard to find within reflections' dance
the ripple's core. What splashed?
Basho's frog, plunked in again?
There is no sound save loud spring wind
that slopes down to mirror-pond and stirs
one twig that sprawls across a fallen branch
and dips just into the center of the ripples
in the mirror and, tip wet, vibrates there.
A twig in wind. A butterfly in China.
How can we know the chaos from the dance?
All I'm sure of in this moment is the pair of dragonflies
flying in the mating wheel around the pond,
releasing tiny eggs round as ripples just above the glass.
Some will fall to minnows, some to larvae, some to mud
to hatch and crawl someday up a stem to split husk
and stretch wings of netted mica round the pond.
One day in wind the larval discard skeleton will
drop from stem and make its ripples there.

Woods Spring

It's not that things are open,
it's that things are opening.
It all unfolds again, croziers of fern
unroll from under soil to light,
their rolled fronds again augur unborn
animals folded in a possum pouch of green,
flower buds unwrap their stars
petal by petal around the wheel
to pinwheel into hearts again,
each time new, impossibly,
we accept again this mood
of opening that's pulled us along
like kids in a toy wagon
since we were new.

Uncracked Egg

On the roadside lies an egg,
large, dried-hay-gold and whole,
sun-warmed, one end a narrow cone,
the other wide and round.
In last night's rain it slipped from
some hungry beak or paw and fell
on this wet indented sand,
cushioned by water
sheeting off the road.
Now it's heavy and warm.
I cup it. Uncracked. Whole.
Is there life inside?
And if so, what then?

Leaf Song

Leaves and light,
light and leaves
never tire our clever eyes,
as if our intuition knows
from first sight
that light plus leaf gives life.

How Words Turn

Hedge bindweed is a noxious weed,
or is it wild morning glory?
Each name says volumes, but
little of the flower: says
how we connect with lives, how not,
how "hedge" calls up landscapes old, but
"bind" speaks to body strange,
how "weed" says unfair competition
and how "noxious" speaks to
the roots of domination,
how "wild" recalls
the Transcendental Earth,
how dawn can wear
the face of glory opening.

A Puzzle for Us Both

The fawn looks back
from the woods
as fawns do,
to see what sent him
leaping to
the safe, tall green.
What kind of thing am I?

No image in his brain
matches me. I am
no running wolf,
no cat bellied down,
I am too new a thing,
a puzzle for us both.

I am new, and fawn is new,
but fawn is elder too,
even with white birth spots
to blend him into dapple.
I have earned no camouflage,
for I am predator wondering
if we will both endure
so long an image grows of me
in fawn's instinctive mind.

What Gives the Beauty Breath

It starts with symmetry, this inhalation
of the senses when they startle purity of form.
These five birdsfoot trefoil blossoms look
identical at first, each rich yellow, each
a pointed dome embraced by yellow skirts,
but then the eye in its delight looks twice
and sees the small asymmetries, petals just ajar
or insect sign, that gives the beauty breath.

Or find the ordinary cinquefoil
set with other perfect roadside weeds,
five petals each indented slightly as a heart, petals
palest butter on the edge, sliding down
a gradient toward a darker center, and mark the twenty
dots of anthers, tan with yellow edges, riding
on brief filaments, but some are blurred, not
quite pollen filled—here the simple cinquefoil
is synonymous with every life on Earth, all
that breathe, with vacuole or stoma, spiracle or lung,
all the slight mismatches that name beauty and are life.

Bird, in Blue

This morning bluebird is serene, entire,
paused in its hunt for bugs
still cold with night
to sit a once-burned branch against a sky
so dense with blue each feather
that is not rust or white
names itself for sky.

If Silver Winks

Kingfisher waits for a silver flash
to reach up from pool,
transfix his eye,
dive him down—

or if silver winks and hides,
kingfisher hovers high in place,
holds his eye in one still space for
that brief gleam, finds it, plummets—
breaks water, wings already strong,
sprinkles rain with
a silver wrinkle in his beak.

Reaching

The growing tip sensitive as finger skin
and motile, extends continually
for something to touch and coil about, this
vegetable movement almost seen but too slow
for our animal eye. Be they nightshade,
creeper, bindweed, pole bean or wild grape, tendrils
reach out, and trust that the stem's
rotation against the sun and a bit of breeze
will blow them into something tangible
to curl about. When they do find touch,
even fleeting, they know it and like
our spirits, curve into shapes of hope,
curves sweet as infants' fingers reaching,
believing that something will be there to hold to.

Bipeds Sunbathing

We are all hot this afternoon, we bipeds,
feathered and bare-skinned.

Five goldfinch males peck about bright shore.
One steps into shallows paved
with smoothed and colored pebbles,
cocks his head at the water
and quick-flutters wings with
wing tips touching water, throws
up drops to spark the light, steps
a little deeper and flutters as he slowly
pivots in a circle. Black feathers
spike upon his crown as wings
wet him down. A rainbow gleam
as drops spray.

I am suddenly the skinny boy I was
splashing in the sandy shallows
at the lake, tossing water
by the hand scoop at my big sister
sunning on the dock.

Circuit made,
the goldfinch stops,

leaps up
and flies to dry upon a bush.

And here I am,
running up the path, afraid
of sisterly revenge,
droplets drying on my skin.

Side by Side

The striped ground squirrel
stands straight upright
to track my intrusion
on his prairie patch.
I am demolished by his charm,
grass-blade gleams, fur tapestry
of lines and spots,
delighted by his forepaws
held out before him as if in appeal, held
side by side, bright with sun, long toes
held like fingers closed.
Were they loose before he saw me?

Wanting Them to Ring

Wild columbine has hung her bells out to rain,
her gold-topped foolscap bells
that ring the child inside
awake
who woke with them in forest clearings
in his true spring lost in time,
who remembers wanting them to ring,
and knows now that they did.

Water-falling

Once long ago, sun spilling wavelets,
I curled my skinny self around
a river stone and fell backwards
out of the rowboat, held my mask tight.
How quickly dark it was, dropping through
that whiskey-watered border lake. I was
glad to embrace warm stone.
How grand to curl up like an ammonite
in ancient seas, swim among fossils.
Like the embrace of ammonite and nautilus,
I want to grow a spiral of my life.
But it takes so long to embrace yourself,
so long to grow larger each segment.
I wish I were still as curly dumb and smart
as that fool kid who fell deep into dark
water and came thrashing up to light.

Pueblo Sun

At Taos Pueblo,
a door, adobe wall, a ladder,
a mop, a dog asleep.
Sun.
The mop put out to dry
drapes a post.
Behind the ladder,
a window, turquoise trim,
white curtain.
Beside the ladder the plain
six-board door,
brown-gray.
The black dog sleeps on his side
in front of the door,
near his head a hand-sized wedge of rock.
Branch rungs on the ladder
through-mortised into juniper uprights
and wedged.
Like all the Taos ladders,
one upright is taller by a foot.
Asymmetric. Wise for climbing down,
a post to hold while
your foot swings out to find the rung.

The dog has found his shade,
the mop its place to dry,
the door has found its weathering,
the ladder knows what it is doing,
and sun has found and made it all.

To Tilt Up

I watch a red-tailed hawk laze up a thermal,
climb spirals of clear air with small effort.
I envy this bird's climb. Spirals are not
just gyres. They ascend, descend,
lift and fall. I'd rather climb the hawk's spiral
than pull ribbons around eternal maypoles.
I know we live in circles rutted with repeating feet,
but I want my circles to tilt up, somewhat like my mind
or lazing skull. I don't want a spiral staircase
to a child's heaven, gates and all,
just now and then a sense that I do climb.

Spirals can twine round each other,
as do vines and DNA, embraced as braids woven tight in hair.
Constraint as embrace, yet together strong.
Too tight hurts. I've seen ironwood trees
twist up toward light together, each
supporting each; watched
an autistic girl slowly twirl her hand and arm
up a thin invisible tree, bend back
her wrist and strike like a snake at
something hidden, over and over again.

The hawk has dwindled to a speck
which is lost. Imagine—to climb a spiral
until you lift beyond sight.

WITH MOUTHS OPEN WIDE

Up from Death

From soil's crucible they rise,
these tender moons, these fruits
of dark that break death down
to grow fruits strange as the pull
of moon upon the blood, as dunes
of tide roll unseen around the salty
yearning ocean Earth
that hears from dry lands the howls
of wolves and women to the moon
who owns no man upon her face.

Swallows Take the Sky

Now toward dusk when wind falls
and insects fly near ground,
a great swim of swallows takes the sky,
whole barn-swallow families
that have left the mud behind.

Swallows skim the tops of grasses
and soybeans, curve up
as if lifting to a wave, swing
round trees and back along the field.
Swallows arc through invisible fluid
as fish dart to invisible prey
above green reefs, jink left, jink right
for flies, mouths wide.
More than half are fledglings. Think:
to first know sky within
a swim of swallows.

The Mushroom Seeks No Light

A tree stands, trunk dark
in light that grows
as golden leaves fall down.
Out of bark
juts one mushroom,
purest white.
Its stem bends sharp upright
as if toward sun.
This mushroom seeks no light
but turns its parasol
against the pull of gravity,
against the rain
that ruins spores.
Mushrooms may not know much,
but unlike some
they do know down from up.

North Country

A small meadow-hawk with eyes
the red of blown coals
perches on a broken branch
to take the sun,
I hope already fed, or
too weary now to fly more
toward its season's end.

Summer spins down and with it
the common multitude of lives
which have dropped their eggs in ponds,
inserted them in soil or stem,

or flowered to sail seed on wind
or made seed prickly so a raccoon
will carry it in fur for days until long fingers
winkle it out and plant it where it lands,

or grew a fruit to carry seed
and timed its sweet so migrating birds
will drop etched seed upon a distant field.

None of this concerns
the little red-eyed dragonfly
whose naiads prowl the pond,
whose coals will wink out soon and cool.

Form Falling

Matter must seek form
as the eye seeks pattern. If
not, why so much patterned
beauty of chaos born? Today,
calm pond grasses bend
flat green on the surface
in bands half a finger wide.
Duckweed punctuates dark water
between leaves dropped
from pondside maples.
Beyond the fallen, patches of dark
balance these bright leaves.
One leaf lies submerged, face down,
one curls up all three points as if
away from water cold, one
blends red with gold. Together green
pond-grass veins and duckweed
lobes set the leaves as gems
above volumes of dark below.

Crucible of Mouths

On my knees, I push leaves
away from soil
they will enter. Everything
is under here, all that life has shed:
acorns, caps, snail shell, seeds,
mushrooms, twigs.
The threads of fungi work
the silence when the crackling stops,
the quiet of autumn's promise.
The goal is to dissolve again,
burn down to basic stuff as this duff has
almost since forever,
and feed the billion pale mouths
that seethe below sight here in
this crucible where earth and air
meet to cycle soil again, again, again.

Autumn Pasture

A fencepost, a vine, green pasture, a hill.

The post is gray with rain
split with time
and slightly out of true.

The vine is autumn red
and next week brown,
records a life of reaching
out beyond the post it's climbed.

The pasture green
insists on growth
beyond the final cutting.

And the hill so green, stretched
all the way to sky calls out
for feet to climb again,
to press turf down and spring.

Driftwood

Mist refuses light, these
nanospheres so lately sea.
If driftwood dreams, light
and lifting are its memories.
Mist and driftwood,
sister, brother to the ocean beach,
endless, without boundary,
earthwide they speak to human hearts
of what is almost known, of
drift and light and dream.

Wei Wu Wei on Lassen Peak

At altitude, on the slopes
of an old volcano, there lives
a grasshopper who follows the Tao.
He does without doing, almost
Is without Being,
so adeptly volcanic his way.
His colors and patterns all
belong to the rock he lives upon,
which he cryptically does
without doing.

The Bird Inside the Heart

At the coffee shop
a woman at the next table
waves a sheet of X-rays
at her friend,
"See? Right there. You
can see the eye.
I have a bird inside my heart."

Maybe that's the difference.
Or maybe we all have birds
inside our hearts, men
and women both, but
some don't get to sing. Or
maybe there are many
lives inside the human heart.
I know a poet with
a woman for a heart, another
has a horse in his that kicks.

No, we must all have birds.
They start small, like us,
grow into difference, like us.
Some know many songs, and sing.
Some know only one, but
do sing, and sing it true.
Some heart birds are mute, can't
sing and never fly, some leap up
and fly everywhere, for the heart
is vast inside and has a sky.

Icicle

I would not mind
growing as I melt.
Must I learn to
corrugate my length
with each shift of cold air?
All the more smooth rolls to gleam.

But suppose I learn
to let go of
what is too much,
learn to bleed
a path toward clear.
Below me, ice will
mound up toward my tip
in my brief and sunbright cave.

This Velvet in the Dark
(New Work)

I. Ring

A Woman and the Architecture of Moon

She doesn't like it. Moon is too present, too
here in all these country windows, where
trees net Moon instead of the exact blot of buildings.
Here night waters double Moon. And fields here
hold a white path to carry the eye up.
City glass is blind at night. Country windows
look out and bring things in. Moon here
looms ever in skylights, whatever the phase it is full.
Moon plucks at her like a hand
plucks a sleeve, a constant, nagging pressure from
someone to forget, the handpluck of a child
she was once responsible for, but not now.
"Hey, Woman," Moon says, pulling, "It's me. Remember?"
She drowns in the old tides and knows herself.
After her womb was removed, she lived
in the city where night blinds are drawn.
Even there, it was never Moon silvering the garden
that baited her, but the sight of its body. And here
with the trees, fields, in the old surround,
Moon's body hangs massive in the sky,
asking, "Woman? Have you forgotten? It's time."

Moon in Synchrony

Moon was always beauty.
How many times at the lake
sitting by her dropped bike
the girl watched Moon's light
cross water to her in that dream-drowse
of summer night when she first
knew it would not get
better than this——but

did sense in that still white
rippling its soft arcs toward her
through the wake of ducks
and through the wave-slapped
sailboats tethered like her
summer eyes, that this
beauty was at once also
the fear pebbling
the backskin of her neck.
Would be brief.
Would be taken.

A Woman, a Circle

She watched her parents and the world and grew
a belief, or maybe heard it somewhere.
At ten, she would try it out in words in bed before sleep.
"When you grow up, your heart dies."
She wasn't sure what she meant, but she believed.
Would not grow up. As she did grow from girl
toward woman, she found in her godmother's
antique store a ring without a stone, a gold band
with an empty three-pronged setting
which she named Ring and wore for years.
She imagined the prongs clasping a pearl,
a small milky moon to stare into. The prongs
reached sharp to her: "Fill me, and your heart will live."
She wore the prongs sometimes out, sometimes twisted in.

Prongs turned in, Ring cut the man's back while
they made love. He asked, as he had
wished: "Your ring . . . ?" She couldn't say.
Her face grew sad, his face. Ring bloodied him again.
She hid it away. Her finger still felt it. Felt it
most when the moon bloodied her.
When she married her love, she didn't want

a child. Oh, she did . . . not yet. Afraid a child would
watch them and grow her belief.

Years since she hid Ring away, her finger still longed.
The circle wouldn't tan. She looked for it after washing up.
When the doctor said "Tumor . . . you can never bear,"
she knew the prongs would not be filled. All that white
winter Ring enclosed the woman and her man. The truth
about circles, she thought: closed, the center
empty. And circles everywhere.

A Woman Emptied

Waiting room all glassed
and smooth, relatives
clumped in chairs, preparing
for the distance of doctors' words.
A few kids run from inside to where
outside crab apples bloom.
In and out. In and out.
The woman is cut open somewhere
upstairs, her head lolls on the table.
One girl through the glass balances
her doll in a bower of branches
filled with pink flowers.
The woman's lover watches from a chair.
The doll is almost too heavy, the girl
catches it, shifts it until it stays.
A soft spring rain.
Kids stand beneath the rainshield,
face the waiting room, press
their lips against the glass.
Running from outside
to inside, the girl tugs, wants
Mom to see. The doll
cannot be borne on flowers
unless someone affirms.
Her fabric face darkens
with the weight of rain.

Dead End

The doctor explains her vagina
is sewn shut at the end, is
now a sort of closed purse
or pocket instead of a path that
led everywhere but explains it
will still be sensitive, smiles, and she,
wordsick, makes pictures of

hollow bird bones, and a sort
of cave which dead-ends, a bright-
lit cave in which she can
no longer become found
or lost, a crater hollow and white
and void of mysteries like

life and the promise of life, like
the thousand more things that
go nowhere, choked closed now.
Like her new purse.

Woman Becomes Moon

She no longer fears
Moon's light or shadows.
All the blood tug in the world
changes nothing.
She is cold inside
the pearl she once
imagined, almost one
with Moon and no more
gender than chalk,
neither Huntress
nor the face
of the nursery man.
Airless, inert, her surface
is smooth, the craters inside.
Tides congealed, she is control.
Now what gleams in her is stone.

Dream of the Barren Field

The night is all dark, Moon obscure, stars afire.
The woman appears in a large plowed field
and is abruptly aware of women all about,
the whole field filled with standing women.
They are just visible, wavering
movements, but the voices are many,
the field enormous. Their voices join
to make a rhythm without words,
and as they chant they sway.
Heads lifted, this field of women chant
cold and low to darkened Moon.
It is the song of no womb.
There are no screams, no cries, too late.
The woman's bare feet struggle with ruts
from the plow, but feel no shoots, only clotted soil.
Tilled over and over, this field grows nothing.
Lucid, she breaks rhythm, congratulates herself
for subtle dreaming—barren field!
But she joins the chant again, for she knows
this ritual is new and somehow being forged,
for women have never gathered, never been
in this world before without wombs but not dead.
Moon never appears, but as their chant fills
the night a faint red tinges the sky.
In the morning the woman sits
on the edge of her bed to examine her feet.

II. Alzheimer's Sequence

In memory of

Pearl Tromblee Caddy

Trailing Arbutus

You should have seen her face glow
when someone said "trailing arbutus."
For Mom's whole long life, arbutus
evoked beauty's mystery.
It's a lovely sound, "arbutus."

Do you know what it is?
Under snowed-in trees in pinewoods
the round arbutus leaves are evergreen.
It trails along in dropped needles with its cousins
bearberry and wintergreen and prince's pine.

Arbutus rings in new spring with small pink trumpet bells.
Should you scent them you would hear them,
and your face too would glow
when a voice said "arbutus."

For Mom, arbutus was a key
to a Time, maybe one magic day, maybe
all one spring, when she and her love were joyed
of life, found in their love and lost.
Had she known how brief,
it would not matter and does not.
She did have her Time, and always after
until this defilement,
arbutus reached into it and made her glow.

Wingflutters

In early summer with luck you catch clothesline and lilac-bush vignettes of fledgling birds begging to be fed. Insistent loud chirps. You have to respond. The main thing is the way they crouch low and stretch their wings out in a fluttering that is comic and almost us, whining kids—but sometimes it flirts that edge, young boys bullied by older, or captives pleading. But that's projection, and this is simply the way young birds beg. Once I found one of the cats attacking a spotbreast robin, and she let me scare her off. The bird was all ajar and twisted in flowers. I couldn't tell how bitten it was but the eyes were shocked bright, the heart visibly pounding. When I reached in, it scuttled spread-winged into the low vincas all disheveled, and panted there, beak open, and fluttered its wings, begging in the only way it knew, and it kept this up, but the only gift came later when it finally lay still.

In the house of relatives, my mother sat little in a stuffed chair while everything whirled about her, confused. She had one spell, the swollen heart racing, her mouth open, gasping, and everyone rushing to get the nitro under her tongue. Then she forgot that. She would smile, flirt a little with the men, open her arms to grandchildren, in between stretches of unsure staring. Talk all around and about her. Now and then she would rouse and ask for her husband, to be told he'd passed away, or had gone on. "Oh? But where is he?" she'd say, and "How long will he be gone?" And told he had died, that he was dead, direct words, her face twisted "Oh no," and wept and was lost. But in a while that closed loop of unmemory would turn again, and she'd smile at the people, coquette the men, stare brightly about, then shrink to dull staring. And all of us helpless.

The morning of my father's funeral, walking in the rain forest, I found a red-shafted flicker on the path. It was adult, in full plumage but unable to fly, and skittered away just under ferns and devil's club. I wanted to help. When I bent to it, the bird opened its beak and opened its wings and silently fluttered. I pulled my hand back.

Moccasin Flower

It was a wistful day, moving in and out of frustration but mostly,
this early day, wistful. She was old and ambiguous and angry
because she knew she was being cheated by Alzheimer's but couldn't
remember of what. Memory was mostly still intact. But in this
reminiscing voice today she revealed an emptiness—not a large one, a
small hole in her life—she said with surprise that she had never seen a
moccasin flower.

I have seen so many, pinks among the heaths and dry jackpine,
    yellows
in the upland poplar, showies in the cedar swamps, rooted in
    sphagnum.
I was astonished she hadn't, all her time in the woods.
What can you do with admissions of holes in our lives?
We all carry them; we abide.

For myself I was returning to a green cathedral space in the woods
I had not seen for thirty years and wasn't sure I could find, if it still
existed at all. It was a place where I changed, and remember growing,
a sphagnum and cedar bog downhill from one of our old
    blueberry spots,
the one where I'd picked around a stump to face off with a bear.
I remember dark columns lifting to green arches in glorious light.
I almost remember that scared, opening boy.

I found the turnoff and the old logging trail. Had to walk the
    last mile.
The place was whole. Green light spilled on hummocks of sphagnum
and leaning trunks. When I hopped from mosstrunk to hummock
    into
that green, I came right to a glory of twenty or thirty pink
    moccasins, full-
flowered in the moss, roots wet, growing in the wrong delightful
    place.

It was more right than wrong to dig one, so I did, and wrapped
    in my shirt
I carried it to where she sat old and heart-fluttered and confused.
Such a smile. And now she had seen a moccasin flower. For now
    she was
a little less empty. One "I never" was gone. And it was good.

It is here I place my faith in earth: there is a green cathedral space
that blessed my mother, and grew me again, and changed itself
to grow pink moccasins.

Dementia

All the old lore speaks of woman in threes:
virgin, mother and crone.
The circle of life's moon:
wax to fullness to wane.
All the stories break woman in three.
Mother breaks into four.

She takes the iron line of her life and
bends it round to the shape without end,
tries to force the moon whole:
the crone tries to marry the virgin,
unbinds her thin hair and shakes
demented magic on the girl she was,
who arrives, eyes casting wild, *Who are you?*
Moon whole—then broken—whole—the
crone's eyes flash hard in the girl's, strobing
here—gone—again here, the marriage

compelled, virgin and crone melt together and sing,
Who's that coming down the tree? Who will marry, marry me?
Ha-ha-ha, you and me, little brown jug don't I love thee . . .
The fit is hard, her hands sway in this mad soft-shoe,
now smiling, now weeping, together they sing,
She can bake a cherry pie in the twinkling of an eye,
but she's a young thing and cannot leave her mother . . .

The crone's eyes flash hard, moon waxes large,
the girl grows afraid, breaks away,
moon gently explodes and huge white chunks
cartwheel off into the old woman's night.
I told them they'd break my wings . . .
Her eyes flash hard, alone: *I know you.*
You get out of here. You get out of here.

Seriously as an Animal

This woman laughed her way out of pain all her life, stood
a moment outside of self and laughed from her belly to her tears but

now she takes herself seriously as an animal—
the hiss of an interrupted cat, the eye-rolled doe who lifts her throat
above the dogs, a grizzled fur who gnaws on iron or just
an old bewilderment tied to a bed where

when she hears a laugh in her room—her daughter's laugh, a
grandson's—she takes herself to be an animal laughed at,
eyes flash and muscles surge but will not lift her to attack, she pants
collapsed like an animal

who cannot lift outside herself or in to find her laugh,
and her children can no longer lift themselves to find their own.

Song Lasts

She's lost language now, words gone
and no sign she cares.
But if you start a song
she knew as a girl,
she will pick it up and sing
clear and strong
as her old voice allows,
lyrics and all—
Daisy, Daisy, give me your answer true . . .
but no sign she cares.
When the song is done it is done.
Think of this, though, through grief—
the song lasts past the mind.
This is not a bad thing to know.

Andrea's Tears

Time is memory,
and when memory is lost
the aged fall out of time,
and for them we weep, within time.
We weep before when we suspect,
we weep when time falls from the mind,
we weep when flesh follows mind,
we weep again after we have wept.
The tears are strange in their falling out of time.

III. Stroke

Stroke: Opening

There are moments of true opening
like the moment in a great aria when
a fine voice descending the scales opens
impossibly and the world is suddenly enlarged, as if
part had been lacking unaware.

Say the plane is descending steeply at flight's end,
your mouth decides to yawn and your ears pop into Here
and sounds are huge and you hadn't
known your ears were closed.

So the plane is descending steeply. And I awake,
step out of bed, and I am suddenly expanding
on the floor trying to stand. My body thumps back down.
Lin's voice: *John! John! What's wrong!*
My mouth leaks noise.

I am aware of outside, but
I float inside a swelling bubble of astonishment.

I try to stand but scuttle
on the floor like an animate question mark.

Inside, enormous space rushes out all around.
I center blackness, this dark entire but

welcome as sable fur to skin.
No fear—in this opening, I am all glad surprise.
Everything is enormous and rushing outward—
Size is all potential; everything is becoming,
everything can happen!

Lin is trying to stand me up.

Back into the question mark.

Emergency

2:30 a.m., May 10, 1994,
Emergency Room, Chisago Hospital

I am an emergency.
Treat me! Help!
My tongue is thick,
my lips don't work.
Night nurse Cathy pulls out a form.
Questions:
Meds, smoke, drink?
Prozac, yes, a couple
margaritas before bed.
Don't you know better than that?
You can't drink with Prozac!

Outraged, she stands to yell
at me in the wheelchair.
Her vehemence confuses.
The attending walks over,
tells her the drinks
have nothing to do with my stroke.
But she knows what she knows,
which young doctors don't.
She is all tight eyes, but quiet.

Four days later, just before
I transfer to Sister Kenney,

night nurse Cathy enters my room,
stays by the door. Her mouth
makes little bitter twists,
"This isn't over yet, you know."

I am amazed at her ill-wishing
from beneath a nurse's cap.
"This isn't over yet."
I know.

Comeback

In Emergency, waiting
for them to do anything,
suddenly I recover. I can speak,
I can move. Not paralyzed. I'm okay!
I tell everyone, maybe yell.
No one seems impressed but me.
But when I unbuckle from the wheelchair, and stand,
they quickly rally round to strap me back.
And like a finger snap, recovery goes away.
Thick tongue, hand clawed.
I overhear the doctor saying to my wife, "TIA,
transient (something) attack."
They have a name, but
they don't have a clue.

Third Person

In Emergency I get my first taste
of voices talking about me as if I've vanished.
My wife and doctor discuss,
and I have suddenly become a thing
called patient—but I'm not,
I call out, try to say, *Hey people,*
I'm right here! Talk to me!
But it's all garble and gargle.
I am a thinking thing that can't talk,
infantilized
in a wheelchair in Emergency.

Left

Loud heparin pump, tubes,
confused. First night waking, dark.
Someone messing with my feet
under the covers.
Okay, John, can you wiggle your right foot?
I want to help. I wiggle it.
Okay, now wiggle your left.
Wha'?
Your left foot. The one I'm holding.
Wiggle your left!
She makes no sense.
I don't know what she means,
or why she keeps repeating "left."
Don't know that no-sense word.
Heparin pump loud. Tubes into me.
I do want to help.
I don't know what she means.

Ward Celebrity

My new doctor knows my name;
he owns a book of mine.
He is excited to have me
in his stroke ward. Strange.
I am briefly a sensation.
The doctor gifts me a book
by Oliver Sacks, *The Man Who
Mistook His Wife for a Hat.*
Oliver looks like my dear
psychiatrist friend who died,
the beard and knowing smile;
I like Oliver's book.
I like my doctor too.

Moan

So I'm in the dark. It's loud here
with breathiness, must be alive.
I find my bewilder here: Stroke Ward.
Night centers down the corridor,
moans loud and long, at times canine,
at times a man who begs Oh, let me die.
Then the loud, long, wordless moan.
My ward is all awake with him—all half-dead we are
and not convinced the other half's alive,
and hang upon this night-moan new guy
who hopes he will stroke out—
that's nurse talk—stroke out.
Hard-heeled, the duty nurses
walk in and out within this tiring moan.
His dear wish angers them.

Tattoo

The redheaded night nurse
wants to show me her tattoo.
It's late, lights out, she's brought
a penlight on her rounds.
She's nice. I say, "Yes, please."
She hands me the penlight,
frees her top three buttons
to reveal her right breast
well-cupped in bra except
the top, which wishes to be free.
"A flower," I falter, shining.
"Beautiful. What kind?"
She leans down close until
the old vet in the next bed
asks, "Is something wrong?"
Oh, no.

Intelligence

Say you know a chunk of brain
is dead and floating up there in your skull,
and no neurons pulse there anymore,
no sparks to make the needles jump.

When they put you in the wheelchair
and take you down this day, you think it's for PT, OT, usual.
But they wheel you past the gym to an office
where a young man says he's a doctor,
a neuropsychologist. Say you ask, *A PhD?*
(You've seen the license on the wall.)

And he agrees, says it's time to take some IQ tests
to see what you can do, and you think, *Right,
to see what I can no longer do.* Your new tongue
asks him if he's read Kafka, if he can picture
Gregor with an apple rotting in his side, but
he can't understand, and you can't wrap
your tongue around *Metamorphosis*. What the hell.

So the test is physical, like the old Stanford-Binet,
or was it Wechsler or some inventory thing?
Say you do find stuff you just can't do, the puzzles
he calls visuospatial, and you want to leave
but this bubbling acid wants to fill your mouth
and you're so freaked you can't find the calm

or care to speak—your left arm
leaps up and vibrates fast like stuttering!

You are ashamed. He knows you're stupid now.
When this shrink totes up his score and lifts his eyes,
he wears a patronizing smile,
the one you've learned to know these past weeks.
You have some neural deficits . . . not so bright.
You are suddenly outraged! What's this for?
To take away what's left?

A New Sensorium

For this time, I have no scales.
My senses are reborn.
Now when egrets float into the pond
I feel an odd and angular pang
at the center of their grace,
like seeing girls who are just
becoming doomed to suffer boys.

So I'm out of Rehab on a weekend pass
after a month of city sounds and smells
through a high hospital window.
When I get home to the house in the trees,
green has learned a thousand new names,
and I wheel around in my chair like some damned teenager
with a lump of beauty in my throat.

Remember? You were thirteen, and the earth
was so beautifully intense
your senses fell into one,
and you surrendered and wept
for the way maples spilled light?
It's like that.

On the front steps I keep falling.
I cannot stand up, and Lin and I can't stop laughing.
Saturday night there are fireflies.

Sometimes we catch the other's eye
and just laugh and laugh until tears—
It is lovely and I don't care why.

There is all this velvet in the dark.

Hemiplegia: The Mummy's Curse

In the forties, the Mummy movies were strong magic,
and our play in Kenny Reid's backyard acted out
the scuffle of the Mummy's dragging foot and his reaching arm,
the horrible shed trail of linen bandage scraps and
a clod here and there of dried mummy flesh.
We saw hieroglyphed crypts, sarcophagi, inhaled
the smoke of tanna leaves to activate Kharis.

Among us kids I was the better Mummy,
dragged my leg with more authority,
expressed such yearning for the mortal in my outstretched arm.
My favorite scene to play was that time in one film where
the Mummy blunders into quicksand and slowly sinks,
his stretching hand and tattered fingers last to disappear.
I would slowly, tragically descend below the grass,
courtesy of a small dip in Kenny's yard.

In the Saturday matinee balcony, as we watched the Wolfman lose to
the moon, our skins tightened in despair. Frankenstein didn't
    really mean
to drop the flower girl into the well—we felt with him
her beauty, moaned with him his pain.
The Mummy's fingers curled for even this cursed rebirth.
Horror was then a little more humane.
Like our first swellings into boymen,
these monsters' power was in their ambiguity.

I loved those moments of delicious fear
when Ken would turn and himself become the Mummy—
we knew as children know
that our terror was only practice for life,
where anyone may play the Mummy,
where we don't have to die of fear.

Once out of the wheelchair and returned to time,
as I learned again to walk
I could not resolve why my lurch felt so familiar,
until one day a child's scared face told me.

I don't have the role quite right—
my arm, instead of stretching in its yearning, curls up toward
    my heart,
but my dragging leg is prime.

When I see small children's faces watch me
scrape down the sidewalk toward them, I know I have become
the thing my child-self feared (and loved), so I smile.

Fallen in the Garden

I lie unquiet on soil I've just enriched
with mined sphagnum, bone meal and dried blood,
toppled off my knees, absurd, collapsed,
earth fragrance stirring in my nose.
At first I strain and twist across the garden bed,
and quit cheek-nestled in the loam, pull
my good hand out from under my leg and squeeze a ball
of earth, hold it on my palm and bring it to my nose.
Not bad.

"The Greatest Straightness Seems Bent"

Lao Tzu

Born of paradox,
I have returned.

I've become my own koan:
I am the sound
of one hand clapping.

Soon I will become the one
who scrapes the barber's throat.

Oh Zeno, Zeno . . . You can too
get there from here!

The Possession of Beauty

Beauty seizes me now
as lust did in my youth.
It owns its own deliriums,
but they are easier
to translate into joy.

In morning grass, a garden spider's take
on the black-hole graphic grid
curves all my space with light
as it bends the world down
the tunnel where she waits at the stems.

>   *Now wasn't that easy?*
>   *What sucks your breath quickly in?*

Beauty seizes me now. Says,
"Ambush is my middle name.
Do you come here often?"
Her circadian riddles play with my rhythms:
Who dares name the colors?
Who dares look all the way up the sky?

>   *Not me. I'm just lying here*
>   *giggling with my friend.*
>   *How long since you spun till you fell?*

I own my own deliriums.
This morning's hoarfrost seizes
all the quiet things and calls
bright bells right out of them.
They translate into joy.

The Innocent Eye

This the doctors call a deficit
of my part-dead brain:
my eyes are new and now
the eyes I owned at three.
I do recall this fascination with the all.
Everything is worthy,
each sight and sound intrigues.
Earth is ever livelier.

Say I have recovered,
say my stroke released
a way of seeing lost,
an eye for every shade of green,
a path young lives walk open wide
with eyes of innocence.

My veils are torn, habit stripped away
like bandages that cover wounds
gifted me by culture and experience.

A naïf again,
I elude sarcasm's net,
do not perceive attacks.
I am uncut wood,

open to the world,
I do not select well what to see.

Years out, I still see
with a child's intensity
small events unlikely seen before.
Oh, look; Oh, see!
I frighten some,
bore a few with
this gift of death rebirth,
an innocence of eye.

John Caddy is the author of several previous collections of poems, among them *Eating the Sting* (Milkweed Editions, 1986) and *The Color of Mesabi Bones* (Milkweed Editions, 1989), which won a Los Angeles Times Book Prize. *Morning Earth: Field Notes in Poetry* (Milkweed Editions, 2003) was the first published collection of Caddy's daily nature poems, which circulate to thousands of readers around the world. His honors include the Bush Foundation Artist's Fellowship, the Loft/McKnight Award, the Minnesota Book Award, two Minnesota State Arts Board Fellowships, and the Sally Ordway Irving Award for his pioneering work in arts education. In 2001, John was named a Bard of the Cornish Gorseth for his contribution to Cornish literature. He lives in rural Minnesota.

Index of Titles and First Lines

Poem titles are set in italics and first lines in roman, excepting first lines originally set in italics, whose style is maintained here.

WITH MOUTHS OPEN WIDE

With Mouths Open Wide

Index

MORE POETRY FROM MILKWEED EDITIONS

To order books or for more information, contact Milkweed at (800) 520-6455
or visit our Web site (www.milkweed.org).

The Color of Mesabi Bones
John Caddy

Eating the Sting
John Caddy

Morning Earth:
Field Notes in Poetry
John Caddy

Turning Over the Earth
Ralph Black

The Phoenix Gone, The Terrace Empty
Marilyn Chin

Invisible Horses
Patricia Goedicke

The Art of Writing
Lu Chi's Wen Fu
*Translated from the Chinese
by Sam Hamill*

Playing the Black Piano
Bill Holm

Willow Room, Green Door
Deborah Keenan

Music for Landing Planes By
Éireann Lorsung

The Freedom of History
Jim Moore

The Porcelain Apes of
Moses Mendelssohn
Jean Nordhaus

Uncoded Woman
Anne-Marie Oomen

Firekeeper:
Selected Poems
Pattiann Rogers

For My Father, Falling Asleep
at Saint Mary's Hospital
Dennis Sampson

Atlas
Katrina Vandenberg

—Milkweed Editions—

Founded in 1979, Milkweed Editions is one of the largest independent, nonprofit literary publishers in the United States. Milkweed publishes with the intention of making a humane impact on society, in the belief that good writing can transform the human heart and spirit. Within this mission, Milkweed publishes in four areas: fiction, nonfiction, poetry, and children's literature for middle-grade readers.

—Join Us—

Milkweed depends on the generosity of foundations and individuals like you, in addition to the sales of its books. In an increasingly consolidated and bottom-line-driven publishing world, your support allows us to select and publish books on the basis of their literary quality and the depth of their message. Please visit our Web site (www.milkweed.org) or contact us at (800) 520-6455 to learn more about our donor program.

Interior design & typesetting
in Centaur Old Style
by RW Scholes
Printed on acid-free Rolland Enviro paper
(100 percent post-consumer waste)
by Friesens Corporation